DRAMA CLASSICS

THE WAY
OF THE WORLD

by

William Congreve

edited and introduced by
Trevor R. Griffiths

NICK HERN BOOKS
London

A Drama Classic

This edition of *The Way of the World* first published
in Great Britain as a paperback original in 1995
by Nick Hern Books Limited, 14 Larden Road,
London W3 7ST

Copyright in the edition of the text © 1995
Trevor R. Griffiths

Copyright in the Introduction © 1995 Nick Hern Books Ltd

Typeset by Country Setting, Woodchurch, Kent TN26 3TB
Printed by BPC, Hazell Books Limited, Aylesbury HP20 1LB

A CIP catalogue record for this book is available from
the British Library

ISBN 1 85459 198 3

Introduction

William Congreve (1670-1729)

William Congreve was born in Bardsey, Yorkshire, on 24 January 1670. He spent much of his early life in Ireland, and his interest in theatre was probably fuelled by visits to the Smock Alley Theatre when he was a classical scholar at Trinity College Dublin. His family returned to England after the 'Glorious Revolution' of 1688 and he began to read law at the Middle Temple in 1691. The great poet and dramatist John Dryden encouraged his literary career. He and the dramatist Thomas Southerne recommended the young man's first play, *The Old Bachelor*, a comedy in the tradition of Sir George Etherege and William Wycherley, to Drury Lane in 1693. It was a major success, with a phenomenally long run, for its time, of fourteen days.

The Double Dealer (1693), Congreve's second play, was more experimental, serious, and satirical, and less successful – due, Congreve argued, to the audience not understanding what he was trying to do. *Love for Love* (1695) was a more conventional, and more successful, comedy, and then Congreve tried his hand at heroic tragedy with *The Mourning Bride*, in 1697. Heroic tragedy has not worn well and Congreve's effort, unlike his comedies, is seldom revived today.

Although Congreve was only thirty when *The Way of the World* was staged at the Lincoln's Inn Fields theatre in 1700, it effectively marked the end of his career as a dramatist. Dryden states that it 'had but a moderate success', and it seems that Congreve may have been trying to do something too complex for contemporary audiences. He may also have been disheartened by attacks on the supposed immorality of Restoration drama by Jeremy Collier, a disaffected clergyman, whose sonorously titled *A Short View of the Immorality and Profaneness of the English Stage* was published in 1698.

However, Congreve continued in theatrical management at Lincoln's Inn Fields until 1705, when he joined Sir John Vanburgh in managing the Queen's Theatre. He wrote a masque, *The Judgment of Paris* (1701), an opera libretto (*Semele*, printed 1710), and had a hand in *Squire Trelooby*, an adaptation from Molière, with Vanbrugh and William Walsh in 1704. He held a number of government posts, including Secretary for Jamaica, before his death on 19 January 1729.

While Congreve's dramatic work draws heavily on both his classical and his legal training, his personal life offers an illuminating insight into the social realities of his time and the plausibility of the plots of *The Way of the World*. As well as a long standing relationship with the actress Anne Bracegirdle (the original Millamant in *The Way of the World*), Congreve also had an affair with the Duchess of Marlborough. Congreve was (and is) generally assumed to have been the father of the Duchess's daughter, who was born in 1723. Contemporary gossip was silenced by the revelation that the Duke was the executor of Congreve's will. However, the Duchess's will provided for her to be buried near her father in Westminster Abbey, rather than with her husband. Since Congreve had already been buried in the Abbey (at the Duchess's instigation) and since she left her daughter 'all Mr Congreves Personal Estate that he left me', as well as jewels bought with money Congreve had left her, the inference is clear. These legal tactics ensured that the disposition of bodies and legacies matched the realities of life as they had lived it rather than as convention dictated. They also suggest that the legal manoeuvres of *The Way of the World* are more solidly grounded in reality than they might appear to a modern audience.

Restoration Comedy and Restoration Society

Although Congreve was not born until ten years after the Restoration of Charles II to the throne in 1660, and *The Way of the World* was not performed until forty years after that event, it is generally regarded as an example of 'Restoration Comedy'. This term has sometimes been used very loosely to cover almost any comedy written between 1660 and 1737, the date of the Licensing Act that introduced effective pre-production censorship of plays. A modern equivalent might be to call all the dramatists writing from 1956 to the present 'Angry Young Men'. Nevertheless, there is enough common ground between say Sir George Etherege at one end of the period and Congreve and Vanburgh writing at the turn of the eighteenth century – in terms of shared approaches to the business of comedy, to characterisation, motifs and themes – to justify continuing to describe *The Way of the World* as a 'Restoration' comedy.

By 1700 the actual Restoration was a distant memory, but the fact that there had been a Restoration is significant both in specific theatrical terms and in terms of the wider political and social contexts in which theatre operated. When Charles II was invited back as King in 1660, eleven years after his father, Charles I, had been executed by a republican government in 1649, the world had changed. The old social order had been based on a relatively static world view in which wealth and power derived from the ownership of land and where religion, rank and social duty constituted a pyramid of interlocking social obligations. with the King at its apex. But the growth of trade and the rise of a wealthy merchant class had gradually imposed strains which led to the Civil War, the breakdown of the old absolutes and a search for a new order. The very fact that Charles I had been deposed, tried and executed meant that things could never be the same again.

The term 'Restoration' tends to be associated with a vision of the merry monarch surrounded by his spaniels and his bevy of mistresses, including the one-time orange-seller and actress Nell Gwynne, and a general atmosphere of libertinism. However, this grossly oversimplifies the complex interactions of a period which also saw the publication of John Milton's epic poems, John Bunyan's *Pilgrim's Progress*, John Locke's psychology, and Newton's physics – all attempts to map out the terrain of a new world in which old certainties had been displaced by new doubts. By the time Congreve wrote *The Way of the World*, Charles II was dead and his Catholic brother James II had been deposed in the 'Glorious Revolution' of 1688 which placed the staidly Protestant William and Mary on the throne.

Plays had been banned in the republican period of the Commonwealth and the theatres closed down. When they reopened officially at the Restoration there were two significant departures from the past: the old open air amphitheatres such as Shakespeare's Globe were finally abandoned in favour of indoor theatres, and actresses were introduced for the first time to play female roles instead of the trained youths familiar from the Elizabethan and Jacobean theatre. The ending of the ban on organised theatre, the return of monarchical rule and the arrival of actresses encouraged a great sense of release, which expressed itself in the form of a cynical and sophisticated comedy of sexual intrigue. 'Restoration comedies' deal almost obsessively with the sexual behaviour and moralities of a very narrow section of late seventeenth-century society, the fashionable, leisured gentlefolk found in a contemporary London of chocolate houses, parks, fashionable *soirées*, and theatres in which they watched themselves being staged. The plays repeat themes, situations, character types (even actual characters), locations and images in such a down-to-earth manner that critics (though not always audiences) have regularly accused the drama of obscenity and pornographic intent or, alternatively, rescued it from such charges by denying it any connection with reality. By 1700 social conditions had changed considerably from those of 1660, and the satirical excess of the immediate Restoration period was under considerable pressure from both inside and outside the theatre. Early Restoration comedies tend to reflect the turmoil of the times, the feeling that the world doesn't make sense any more, the difficulties of finding a way to reconcile social pressure with personal desire, through satire. Later comedies, including *The Way of the World*, also attempt to suggest ways forward, to reconcile the conflicting desires to protect inherited wealth and to achieve personal fulfilment through love.

The new theatres of the Restoration adopted the kinds of changeable scenery that had been introduced to the English theatre through the elaborate court masques of the early seventeenth century. The scenery was made up of shutters that moved in grooves, so that scene changes consisted of opening and closing these shutters behind the actors. In *The Way of the World*, for example, the painted scenery for the first act would have represented the Chocolate House and would have opened to reveal the next scene, a picture of St James's Park. Actors entered through

doors at either side of the proscenium arch, or from between the
scenery shutters at the side, or, sometimes, were discovered as the
shutters parted, the actors then coming forward onto the large
forestage to act the scene. This meant that, although the performers
still shared the same space as the audience, they were now acting
against a background of pictures that in some way illustrated the
play. Since both the auditorium and the stage were evenly lit
throughout the performance, the audience could see themselves
as well as they could see the actors. This probably added an extra
dimension to the sense of theatre as a reflection of life since the
stage was peopled with characters in the same kind of fashionable
dress as their audience, using contemporary turns of speech, moving
against a background of scenery depicting the world as it might be
found outside the theatre.

What Happens in the Play

Mirabell, who is in love with the heiress Millamant, has been
gaining access to her by pretending to be in love with her aunt,
Lady Wishfort, who controls half of Millamant's fortune. Another
young woman, Mrs Marwood, spurned by Mirabell, has taken
revenge on him by revealing his pretence to Lady Wishfort. If
Mirabell is to marry Millamant, he needs to find a way of forcing
Lady Wishfort, who now hates him, to let him have the fortune.
He therefore sets up a plot in which his servant Waitwell will pass
himself off as Mirabell's uncle Sir Rowland, and make a pretended
marriage to Lady Wishfort. Mirabell will then be able to force Lady
Wishfort to do what he wants, rather than risk the fake marriage
being exposed to public derision. Prudently Mirabell has enlisted
the help of Lady Wishfort's maidservant Foible, and has her
married to Waitwell to prevent any possibility of a double cross.

Earlier Mirabell has also had an affair with Lady Wishfort's daugh-
ter, now Mrs Fainall, who is Millamant's cousin and confidante.
Fainall, her husband, who is himself Mrs Marwood's lover, tells
Lady Wishfort about this affair and Mirabell's plot. He and
Mrs Marwood threaten to make Lady Wishfort a laughing stock
and Fainall threatens to divorce his wife unless he is put in control

of Millamant's fortune as well as his wife's. However, Mrs Fainall proves that her husband and Mrs Marwood are lovers, and Mirabell produces a deed that shows that he is Mrs Fainall's trustee. Fainall's claims on her property cannot be sustained, the villains are discomforted and Lady Wishfort agrees to Mirabell marrying Millamant.

Comedy of Manners, Comedy of Humours, Characterisation

Comedy of Manners is one of the most persistent comic forms. Generally Comedies of Manners are preoccupied with showing the social behaviour of the contemporary rich and leisured class. In the English theatre, there is a virtually unbroken Comedy of Manners tradition from the Restoration through Sheridan and Goldsmith to Boucicault, Wilde, Coward, and Ayckbourn. Sometimes the plays simply reflect their society uncritically, sometimes they are savagely critical of its manners. Many of the finest Comedies of Manners, including *The Way of the World*, explore social codes in ways that lead to a critique of society and the suggestion of modifying those codes to deal with the hypocrisies that the manners can hide.

Congreve drew his inspiration from a variety of previous dramatists as well as from contemporary life. As a classical scholar he knew the plays of the Roman dramatist Terence, which feature young men hunting for legacies. He was also operating within a theatrical tradition that valued the satirical comedy of Ben Jonson, as developed by his own immediate predecessors such as Etherege and Wycherley, more highly than the romantic comedy of Shakespeare. He draws heavily on Jonson's Comedy of Humours for the names of his characters, giving them names that are a guide to dominant facets of their individual characters. Generally the more peripheral and straightforwardly comic characters like Petulant, Mincing, and Witwoud who actually make little impact on the plot are more closely defined by their names and prevailing character traits. Lady Wishfort is a clear exception to this, since her whole comic force depends on her inappropriate wish for an 'iteration of nuptials'.

In his Dedication (pages 2-5), Congreve himself differentiates his methods from contemporary theatre practice. Satirical comedies sometimes targeted the naturally foolish rather than those who affected a greater wit or wisdom than they actually possessed. But Congreve stressed that an audience should react to natural fools reflectively, with compassion and charity, and goes on to say 'this reflection moved me to design some characters which should appear ridiculous not so much through natural folly (which is incorrigible and therefore not proper for the stage) as through an affected wit'. This approach may also reflect Congreve's response to Collier's attacks on the supposed immorality of Restoration drama. Although Congreve's ironic comment within the play is to place Collier's book on Lady Wishfort's shelves as suitably pious reading for his villainess Mrs Marwood, he was stung by Collier, and published a riposte, his *Amendments of Mr Collier's False and Imperfect Citations*, in the same year as Collier's diatribe.

Congreve's satirical attacks on affectation and his use of the Humours tradition in naming characters may have suggested to his original audience that the characters would be caricatures with one broad defining characteristic, and this certainly applies to someone like Mincing with her affected and esoteric pronunciation and vocabulary. While the names of the major characters do reveal less about their whole personalities, they remain important pointers to how we are meant to judge them. For example, it is hard to decide from their initial dialogue alone whether Fainall or Mirabell is to be the play's hero, but their names indicate that we are meant to admire the 'admirable' character and distrust the one who 'feigns all', although the information that gradually emerges about Mirabell makes him a more complex figure than his name might suggest. This refusal to settle for the single viewpoint is an important factor in giving life to the play, but its almost Chekhovian complexity of motivation and allusiveness may have been an element in the initial apparently disappointing response to the play. Of course the characters are partly a product of the generic expectations of Restoration comic form, but we are also asked to make judgments on them as we would in everyday life, and those judgments change as our picture of them builds up gradually throughout the play. So there is a tension at the heart of the play between the generic expectations set up by names like Fainall and Wishfort and the more complex ways in which even some of the minor figures are presented.

Relationships and Structure

Congreve uses juxtapositions of different kinds of relationships as a central part of his dramatic method. His list of 'Dramatis Personae' offers a grid of such descriptions: Fainall is 'in love with Mrs Marwood', Millamant is 'niece to Lady Wishfort and loves Mirabell'. Most complicated of all, Mrs Fainall is 'daughter to Lady Wishfort and wife to Fainall, formerly friend to Mirabell'. Mrs Marwood, who is 'friend to Mr Fainall and likes Mirabell' is a loose cannon who has no family affiliation other than being Fainall's mistress, but otherwise the patterns of kinship and of liking are equally complicated. As Fainall says to Mirabell about Sir Wilfull: 'he is half-brother to this Witwoud by a former wife, who was sister to my Lady Wishfort, my wife's mother. If you marry Millamant you must call cousins too.' In general, the play moves on two planes at once, testing emotional realities against social realities, gradually revealing the discrepancy between underlying emotional commitments and outer social forms and equally gradually suggesting new social forms that might reflect the shifts in emotional commitments.

An example of this is the way in which family relationships are tested in each act against emotional ones. Act One is exclusively male, beginning with a conversation between the two gamblers who are to be at the centre of the plots, in a public arena (the Chocolate House); Act Two, set in the park, another public space, begins with a similar dialogue between the former mistress of one of the gamblers and the current mistress of the other (who also desires the first!). In both dialogues, the participants use hints and evasions to probe each other for signs of weakness and the true state of emotional affairs. Congreve organises matters like a formal dance: after the two scenes in which the Mirabell-Mrs Fainall axis is established against the Mr Fainall-Mrs Marwood axis, we see a further set of juxtaposed scenes in which Fainall and Mrs Marwood (the adulterous couple) are acrimonious, the ex-lovers, Mirabell and

Mrs Fainall, are forgiving, and the current lovers, Mirabell and Millamant, are sparring.

The first two acts reveal discrepancies between external appearances and the underlying relationships in public places. Act Three takes us into the domestic arena of Lady Wishfort's house, where it remains for the rest of the play. Here the central event in the plot, (Mrs Marwood overhearing Foible's discussion with Mrs Fainall) reveals a key discrepancy between outward appearance and the reality that the aristocratic suitor 'Sir Rowland' is actually Waitwell, Mirabell's servant. The rest of the play takes the open grid of relationships between those people who are linked through blood and marriage and the much more secret grid of those who are attached through passion rather than law, and works to rearrange the pattern so that there is a much closer match between the emotional and the legal situation by the end. Legal devices and legal vocabulary become a sustaining dramatic metaphor for human obligations and social relationships.

Love, Marriage and Money

For the aristocracy and gentry who form the Dramatis Personae of *The Way of the World*, and for their contemporaries in the audience, marriage was not primarily, or even necessarily, a matter of romantic attachments between individuals. As Congreve's contemporary the poet Samuel Butler wrote, 'Matrimony's but a bargain made/ To serve the turns of interest and trade;/Not out of love or kindness, but designs/To settle lands and tenements like fines'. The transfer of wealth, property and lands between families was a key factor in determining who married whom, and the romantic inclinations of the bride and groom were often secondary to any dynastic advantages that might arise from a marriage. This led to many loveless relationships and to cynicism about the institution of marriage as a whole.

By concentrating on courtship and marriage, dramatists were able to investigate discrepancies between the social code and underlying emotional realities. In a society effectively without divorce, how could marriage be arranged on anything other than a commercial basis? Many men and women were trapped in unions without affection, and the inevitable results were distrust, jealousy, and contempt. Women had very little independence, and Congreve was reflecting the realities of late seventeenth-century life as much as classical precedent in showing a wealthy heiress being pursued for her inheritance. In real life the practice was so common that some critics have suggested that far from being surprised at Mrs Fainall's financial caution in conveying her estate into Mirabell's care, as we might be, contemporary audiences might have been puzzled at her apparent failure to take precautions against a predatory second husband.

Act Four: the 'Proviso' Scene

Congreve is explicit in insisting that only half Millamant's fortune is under her aunt's control. A real-life Millamant could easily have married on the remaining £6000 that she controls herself. So why are Mirabell's convoluted stratagems actually necessary? They are partly a demonstration of his seriousness as a lover, almost like the test of a medieval knight errant wooing his lady. Since both the Fainalls' existing marriage and the various marriages referred to and proposed within in the play are scarcely models for a genuine union of kindred spirits, the action tests Mirabell's and Millamant's willingness and commitment to undertake such a hazardous enterprise. The underlying question of *The Way of the World* is how the sexes can find a way of living together that is not a purely economic arrangement, but one in which emotional and legal realities match and which is not characterised by excess. It is comic when Millamant says, 'If Mirabell should not make a good husband, I am a lost thing'; the underlying loss is not only an emotional one, but also that of financial independence.

Act Four consists largely of a series of marriage proposals of varying strengths and sincerity. The majority of these proposals are to Millamant, and the majority of her would-be suitors are at best perfunctory. Sir Wilfull, for example, woos her out of duty not love, but is unable to match her town sophistication with his uneducated country manners; Petulant's outburst is brief and brutal. As well as the internal contrast between the various proposals to Millamant, there is a further contrast when romance does appear in the artificially heightened language of Waitwell wooing Lady Wishfort as Sir Rowland. Even Lady Wishfort voices the play's scepticism about the relationship between high-sounding moral absolutes and the realities of *The Way of the World* when she describes Sir Rowland's language as excessive. All these proposals and the Fainalls' marriage offer negative models of the dangers that attend courtship and marriage. They provide a sharp contrast to Mirabell and Millamant's moving comic exorcism of those dangers as they agree mutual terms and ground rules for their marriage in what has come to be called 'the proviso scene' because of the conditions ('provisos') that they lay down for each other.

Although this is not the first such scene in Restoration Comedy, Mirabell and Millamant's declaration of love is a fine example of a typically understated reticent English love scene. The emotional core of their relationship is not expressed directly; instead social forms are made to match emotional reality as the characters use the methods of formal debate and cross-examination to agree a set of conditions for their relationship that allow them the possibility of uniting emotional and legal commitment. In the face of excesses of drunkenness, abruptness, gallantry and inarticulacy, the calm, rational, formal balance of Mirabell's and Millamant's alternating conditions – concisely captured when Mirabell completes Millamant's quoted couplet from a poem by Edmund Waller – appears the most desirable way of living on offer within the world of the play. It is a scene rich in comic possibilities that has been exploited to the full, in this century, by such actresses as Edith Evans, Geraldine McEwan and Maggie Smith, who have revelled in the opportunities that Millamant offers for witty banter and coquetry.

Relationships, Power, Law, and Knowledge

When there is a discrepancy between outward and inner orders, anyone who knows the facts has power over those who do not. Part of the pleasure of watching or reading *The Way of the World* lies in the way that the balance of power between characters and between characters and audience fluctuates depending on who knows what, when, and about whom; with the prizes going to those who can best exploit their knowledge of those discrepancies. This also partly explains the importance of irony and wit in these plays, since verbal control, or lack of it, is not only a source of comedy, but also stands as a kind of metaphor for the social and emotional control exerted by the truly witty characters.

In *The Way of the World* anyone who is aware of a discrepancy has power over others, and the play is organised through a series of revelations and counter-revelations – a peeling away of layers of deceit and misapprehension. In these terms, the play is a power struggle over the control of legacies. Lady Wishfort controls half of Millamant's fortune; Fainall and Mirabell each want to persuade or force Lady Wishfort to make a disposition in their own favour. The conflict is resolved by the appearance of a previously concealed legal document that gives Mirabell power over Mrs Fainall's fortune, in the same way as the marriage between Waitwell and Foible was intended to give Mirabell power over Lady Wishfort. Interestingly, however, in the last act, the revelation of Fainall's affair with Mrs Marwood, which the other characters assume will be actually as well as morally disabling, makes no difference at all to Fainall. He readily accepts the disjunction between the social and emotional order and when he is ultimately defeated, it is not by an action within the play, but by Mirabell's superior knowledge of a state of affairs prior to the play – the trump card of the writings in the black box.

Some Restoration comedies appear both to share Fainall's acceptance of the discrepancy between outward appearance and inner states of affairs and to glorify in it. However, the action of *The Way of the World* involves a sense of cleansing, as the outward expressions of human relationships in the form of marriages and legal documents come to match more fully the inward states of human emotions. It is this that explains the true importance of the deed Mirabell produces at the end of the play. At one level it is no more than a dramatic device to cut through a tightly knotted situation, but it is more than the final hidden secret at the centre of the pattern of revelations about the hidden emotional structures. Since it finally frees the characters who appear to be controlled by Lady Wishfort, it offers a fundamental basis on which to build a new social order.

A Transitional Comedy?

Ultimately *The Way of the World* presents a comic vision of a world beset by doubts and uncertainties, in which individuals must seek their own stability without recourse to external moral systems. Like Shakespeare's *Twelfth Night* and *The Merchant of Venice* it cannot accommodate all its characters within its comic synthesis: Fainall and Mrs Marwood are excluded, and Mrs Fainall's future happiness, if not her wealth, is problematic.

The Way of the World is sometimes seen as marking a transition between the more overtly cynical work of the Restoration proper and what came to be called Sentimental Comedy, in which the characters are sober and their sentiments fine, with the predictable result that the plays tend to be both morally uplifting and deeply dull. Mirabell is almost the last of the Restoration libertines, caught in a process of transition into a sententious (Millamant's accusation) eighteenth-century man of feeling: one could not easily imagine earlier Restoration heroes discussing how to bring up children with their future wives. While Mirabell is no heroic exemplar, he may, as Congreve said of the hero of his earlier comedy *Love for Love*, 'pass well enough for the best character in a comedy'. Yet, while Congreve was referring to the classical tradition that comedy shows human beings as worse than they are, there is something challengingly modern about the vision of *The Way of the World*, with its hero and heroine peering forward into an uncertain world, unsure of their bearings, but witty, resolute, and mutually supportive.

Trevor R. Griffiths

The Text

This edition is based on the 1700 Quarto with spelling and punctuation modernised.

Further Reading

The standard biographical studies are John C. Hodges's *Congreve the Man* (London, 1941) and his *William Congreve: Letters and Documents* (London, 1964). Norman N. Holland's *The First Modern Comedies* (Harvard, 1959) is a thoughtful study of Restoration comedy. Both Peter Holland's *The Ornament of Action* (Cambridge, 1979) and Jocelyn Powell's *Restoration Theatre Production* are fine theatre-centred accounts of Restoration theatre and drama; each has a chapter on *The Way of the World*. Malcolm Kelsall's *Congreve: 'The Way of the World'* (London, 1981) is an incisive, brief study. David L. Hirst's *Comedy of Manners* (London, 1979) remains one of the best accounts of the genre to which *The Way of the World* belongs.

Key Dates

1670 Born in Bardsey, Yorkshire, 24 January.

1674 Brought up in Ireland where his father was in the army.

1681 Attended Kilkenny School, to 1685.

1686 Classical Scholar at Trinity College Dublin.

1688 The 'Glorious Revolution' leads to the family's return from Ireland.

1691 Enters the Middle Temple to train as a lawyer.

1692 Translates Juvenal's Eleventh Satire; publishes *Incognita*, a novel.

1693 *The Old·Bachelor*, a comedy, produced at Drury Lane with great success, achieving the very long run, for its time, of fourteen days.

1693 *The Double Dealer*, a more experimental comedy, produced at Drury Lane with less success.

1695 *Love for Love*, a more conventional comedy, opened the new Lincoln's Inn Fields theatre with a thirteen-day run. Wrote 'An Essay Concerning Humour in Comedy'.

1697 *The Mourning Bride*, a heroic tragedy, produced at Lincoln's Inn Fields.

1697 Manager at Lincoln's Inn Fields, to 1705.

1698 Published *Amendments to Mr Collier's False and Imperfect Citations*, a response to Jeremy Collier's attack on the supposed immorality of the stage in his *A Short View of the Immorality and Profaneness of the English Stage* (1697).

1700 *The Way of the World* staged at Lincoln's Inn Fields.

1701 *The Judgment of Paris*, a masque.

1704 *Squire Trelooby*, an adaptation from Molière, with Vanbrugh and William Walsh.

1705 Managed the Queen's Theatre with Sir John Vanburgh, to 1706.

1710 *Semele*, an opera libretto, printed in his *Works*.

1710 Until his death, held a number of government posts, including Commissioner of Wine Licenses, Undersearcher of Customs, Secretary for Jamaica.

1717 Edited *The Dramatic Works* of Dryden.

1723 Mary Godolphin, daughter of Duchess of Marlborough, born.

1729 Died, on 19 January. Buried in Westminster Abbey.

THE WAY OF THE WORLD

Dedication

TO THE RIGHT HONOURABLE RALPH
EARL OF MOUNTAGUE ETC.

My Lord,

Whether the world will arraign me of vanity or not, that I have
presumed to dedicate this comedy to your Lordship, I am yet in
doubt: though it may be it is some degree of vanity even to doubt
of it. One who has at any time had the honour of your Lordship's
conversation, cannot be supposed to think very meanly of that
which he would prefer to your perusal; yet it were to incur the
imputation of too much sufficiency to pretend to such a merit as
might abide the test of your Lordship's censure.

Whatever value may be wanting to this play while yet it is mine,
will be sufficiently made up to it when it is once become your
Lordship's; and it is my security that I cannot have overrated it
more by my dedication than your Lordship will dignify it by your
patronage.

That it succeeded on the stage was almost beyond my expectation;
for but little of it was prepared for that general taste which seems
now to be predominant in the palates of our audience.

Those characters which are meant to be ridiculous in most of our
comedies are of fools so gross that, in my humble opinion, they
should rather disturb than divert the well-natured and reflecting
part of an audience; they are rather objects of charity than contempt; and instead of moving our mirth, they ought very often to
excite our compassion.

This reflection moved me to design some characters which should
appear ridiculous not so much through a natural folly (which is
incorrigible, and therefore not proper for the stage) as through an

affected wit: a wit, which at the same time that it is affected, is also false. As there is some difficulty in the formation of a character of this nature, so there is some hazard which attends the progress of its success upon the stage. For many come to a play so over-charged with criticism that they very often let fly their censure, when through their rashness they have mistaken their aim. This I had occasion lately to observe; for this play had been acted two or three days before some of these hasty judges could find the leisure to distinguish betwixt the character of a Witwoud and a Truewit.

I must beg your Lordship's pardon for this digression from the true course of this epistle; but that it may not seem altogether impertinent, I beg that I may plead the occasion of it, in part of that excuse of which I stand in need for recommending this comedy to your protection. It is only by the countenance of your Lordship, and the few so qualified, that such who write with care and pains can hope to be distinguished, for the prostituted name of poet promiscuously levels all that bear it.

Terence, the most correct writer in the world, had a Scipio and a Lelius, if not to assist him, at least to support him in his reputation; and notwithstanding his extraordinary merit, it may be their coun-tenance was not more than necessary.

The purity of his style, the delicacy of his turns, and the justness of his characters, were all of them beauties which the greater part of his audience were incapable of tasting; some of the coarsest strokes of Plautus, so severally censured by Horace, were more likely to affect the multitude; such who come with expectation to laugh out the last act of a play, and are better entertained with two or three unseasonable jests, than with the artful solution of the fable.

As Terence excelled in his performances, so had he great advan-tages to encourage his undertakings, for he built most on the foundations of Menander: his plots were generally modelled, and his characters ready drawn to his hand. He copied Menander; and Menander had no less light in the formation of his characters from the observations of Theophrastus, of whom he was a disciple; and Theophrastus, it is known, was not only the disciple but the immediate successor of Aristotle, the first and greatest judge of poetry. These were great models to design by; and the further advantage which Terence possessed towards giving his plays the due ornaments of purity of style, and justness of manners, was not less considerable from the freedom of conversation which was permitted him with Lælius and Scipio, two of the greatest and most polite men of his age. And indeed, the privilege of such a conversation is the only certain means of attaining to the perfection of dialogue.

If it has happened in any part of this comedy that I have gained a turn of style or expression more correct, or at least more corrigible than in those which I have formerly written, I must, with equal pride and gratitude, ascribe it to the honour of your Lordship's admitting me into your conversation, and that of a society where everybody else was so well worthy of you, in your retirement last summer from the town, for it was immediately after that this comedy was written. If I have failed in my performance, it is only to be regretted, where there were so many not inferior either to a Scipio or a Lelius, that there should be one wanting equal to the capacity of a Terence.

If I am not mistaken, poetry is almost the only art which has not yet laid claim to your Lordship's patronage. Architecture, and painting, to the great honour of our country, have flourished under your influence and protection. In the mean time, poetry, the eldest sister of all arts, and parent of most, seems to have resigned her birthright by having neglected to pay her duty to your Lordship, and by permitting others of a later extraction to prepossess that place in your esteem to which none can pretend a better title. Poetry, in its nature, is sacred to the good and great; the relation between them is reciprocal, and they are ever propitious to it. It is the privilege of poetry to address to them, and it is their prerogative alone to give it protection.

This received maxim is a general apology for all writers who consecrate their labours to great men. But I could wish at this time that this address were exempted from the common pretence of all dedications; and that, as I can distinguish your Lordship even among the most deserving, so this offering might become remarkable by some particular instance of respect, which should assure your Lordship that I am, with all due sense of your extreme worthiness and humanity,

My LORD,

Your Lordship's most obedient and most obliged humble servant,

WILL. CONGREVE.

6

Dramatis Personae

Men
FAINALL, *in love with* MRS MARWOOD
MIRABELL, *in love with* MRS MILLAMANT
WITWOUD,
SIR PETULANT, } *followers of* MRS MILLAMANT
WILFULL WITWOUD, *half-brother to* WITWOUD,
    and nephew to LADY WISHFORT
WAITWELL, *servant to* MIRABELL

Women
LADY WISHFORT, *enemy to* MIRABELL, *for having falsely*
    pretended love to her
MRS MILLAMANT, *a fine lady, niece to* LADY WISHFORT,
    and loves MIRABELL
MRS MARWOOD, *friend to* MR FAINALL, *and likes* MIRABELL
MRS FAINALL, *daughter to* LADY WISHFORT, *and wife to*
    FAINALL, *formerly friend to* MIRABELL
FOIBLE, *woman to* LADY WISHFORT
MINCING, *woman to* MRS MILLAMANT

Dancers, Footmen, and Attendants

The scene: London

The time: equal to that of the presentation

Prologue

Spoken by Mr Betterton.

Of those few fools, who with ill stars are cursed,
Sure scribbling fools, called poets, fare the worst;
For they're a sort of fools which Fortune makes,
And after she has made 'em fools, forsakes.
With Nature's oafs 'tis quite a different case,
For Fortune favours all her idiot race;
In her own nest the cuckoo eggs we find,
O'er which she broods to hatch the changeling kind.
No portion for her own she has to spare,
So much she dotes on her adopted care.

Poets are bubbles, by the town drawn in,
Suffered at first some trifling stakes to win;
But what unequal hazards do they run!
Each time they write, they venture all they've won;
The squire that's buttered still, is sure to be undone.
This author, heretofore, has found your favour,
But pleads no merit from his past behaviour.
To build on that might prove a vain presumption,
Should grants to poets made admit resumption;
And in Parnassus he must lose his seat,
If that be found a forfeited estate.

He owns, with toil he wrought the following scenes,
But if they're naught ne'er spare him for his pains;
Damn him the more; have no commiseration
For dullness on mature deliberation.
He swears he'll not resent one hissed-off scene,
Nor, like those peevish wits, his play maintain,
Who, to assert their sense, your taste arraign.

Some plot we think he has, and some new thought;
Some humour too, no farce; but that's a fault.
Satire, he thinks, you ought not to expect;
For so reformed a town, who dares correct?
To please this time has been his sole pretence;
He'll not instruct, lest it should give offence.
Should he by chance a knave or fool expose,
That hurts none here; sure here are none of those.
In short our play shall (with your leave to show it)
Give you one instance of a passive poet.
Who to your judgments yields all resignation;
So save or damn, after your own discretion.

ACT ONE

Scene One

A chocolate-house.

MIRABELL *and* FAINALL *rising from cards.* BETTY *waiting.*

MIRABELL. You are a fortunate man, Mr Fainall.

FAINALL. Have we done?

MIRABELL. What you please. I'll play on to entertain you.

FAINALL. No, I'll give you your revenge another time, when you are not so indifferent; you are thinking of something else now, and play too negligently. The coldness of a losing gamester lessens the pleasure of the winner. I'd no more play with a man that slighted his ill fortune, than I'd make love to a woman who undervalued the loss of her reputation.

MIRABELL. You have a taste extremely delicate, and are for refining on your pleasures.

FAINALL. Prithee, why so reserved? Something has put you out of humour.

MIRABELL. Not at all. I happen to be grave today, and you are gay; that's all.

FAINALL. Confess, Millamant and you quarrelled last night after I left you. My fair cousin has some humours that would tempt the patience of a Stoic. What, some coxcomb came in and was well received by her, while you were by?

MIRABELL. Witwoud and Petulant; and what was worse, her aunt, your wife's mother, my evil genius; or to sum up all in her own name, my old Lady Wishfort came in.

FAINALL. Oh there it is then! She has a lasting passion for you, and with reason. What, then my wife was there?

MIRABELL. Yes, and Mrs Marwood, and three or four more whom I never saw before. Seeing me, they all put on their grave faces, whispered one another; then complained aloud of the vapours, and after fell into a profound silence.

FAINALL. They had a mind to be rid of you.

MIRABELL. For which reason I resolved not to stir. At last the good old lady broke through her painful taciturnity with an invective against long visits. I would not have understood her, but Millamant joining in the argument, I rose and with a constrained smile told her, I thought nothing was so easy as to know when a visit began to be troublesome. She reddened and I withdrew, without expecting her reply.

FAINALL. You were to blame to resent what she spoke only in compliance with her aunt.

MIRABELL. She is more mistress of herself than to be under the necessity of such a resignation.

FAINALL. What? Though half her fortune depends upon her marrying with my lady's approbation?

MIRABELL. I was then in such a humour that I should have been better pleased if she had been less discreet.

FAINALL. Now I remember, I wonder not they were weary of you; last night was one of their cabal nights; they have 'em three times a week, and meet by turns at one another's apartments, where they come together like the coroner's inquest, to sit upon the murdered reputations of the week. You and I are excluded; and it was once proposed that all the male sex should be excepted; but somebody moved that to avoid scandal there might be one man of the community; upon which motion Witwoud and Petulant were enrolled members.

MIRABELL. And who may have been the foundress of this sect? My Lady Wishfort, I warrant, who publishes her detestation of mankind, and full of the vigour of fifty-five, declares for a friend

and ratafia, and let posterity shift for itself, she'll breed no
more.

FAINALL. The discovery of your sham addresses to her, to
conceal your love to her niece, has provoked this separation.
Had you dissembled better, things might have continued in the
state of nature.

MIRABELL. I did as much as man could, with any reasonable
conscience; I proceeded to the very last act of flattery with her,
and was guilty of a song in her commendation. Nay, I got a
friend to put her into a lampoon, and compliment her with the
imputation of an affair with a young fellow, which I carried so
far that I told her the malicious town took notice that she had
grown fat of a sudden; and when she lay in of a dropsy,
persuaded her she was reported to be in labour. The devil's in't,
if an old woman is to be flattered further, unless a man should
endeavour downright personally to debauch her; and that my
virtue forbad me. But for the discovery of that amour I am
indebted to your friend, or your wife's friend, Mrs Marwood.

FAINALL. What should provoke her to be your enemy, without
she has made you advances which you have slighted? Women
do not easily forgive omissions of that nature.

MIRABELL. She was always civil to me till of late. I confess I am
not one of those coxcombs who are apt to interpret a woman's
good manners to her prejudice, and think that she who does
not refuse 'em everything, can refuse 'em nothing.

FAINALL. You are a gallant man, Mirabell; and though you may
have cruelty enough not to satisfy a lady's longing, you have too
much generosity not to be tender of her honour. Yet you speak
with an indifference which seems to be affected, and confesses
you are conscious of a negligence.

MIRABELL. You pursue the argument with a distrust that seems
to be unaffected, and confesses you are conscious of a concern
for which the lady is more indebted to you than your wife.

FAINALL. Fie, fie, friend, if you grow censorious I must leave you.
I'll look upon the gamesters in the next room.

MIRABELL. Who are they?

FAINALL. Petulant and Witwoud. (*To* BETTY.) Bring me some chocolate.

Exit.

MIRABELL. Betty, what says your clock?

BETTY. Turned of the last canonical hour, sir. (*Exit.*)

MIRABELL. How pertinently the jade answers me! (*Looking on his watch.*) Ha? almost one o'clock! Oh, y'are come –

Enter a SERVANT.

Well, is the grand affair over? You have been something tedious.

SERVANT. Sir, there's such coupling at Pancras that they stand behind one another, as 'twere in a country dance. Ours was the last couple to lead up, and no hopes appearing of dispatch, besides the parson growing hoarse, we were afraid his lungs would have failed before it came to our turn; so we drove round to Duke's Place, and there they were riveted in a trice.

MIRABELL. So, so, you are sure they are married.

SERVANT. Married and bedded, sir; I am witness.

MIRABELL. Have you the certificate?

SERVANT. Here it is, sir.

MIRABELL. Has the tailor brought Waitwell's clothes home, and the new liveries?

SERVANT. Yes, sir.

MIRABELL. That's well. Do you go home again, d'ye hear, and adjourn the consummation till farther order. Bid Waitwell shake his ears, and Dame Partlet rustle up her feathers, and meet me at one o'clock by Rosamond's Pond, that I may see her before she returns to her lady; and as you tender your ears, be secret.

Exit SERVANT.

Re-enter FAINALL.

FAINALL. Joy of your success, Mirabell; you look pleased.

MIRABELL. Ay. I have been engaged in a matter of some sort of mirth which is not yet ripe for discovery. I am glad this is not a cabal night. I wonder, Fainall, that you who are married, and of consequence should be discreet, will suffer your wife to be of such a party.

FAINALL. Faith, I am not jealous. Besides, most who are engaged are women and relations; and for the men, they are of a kind too contemptible to give scandal.

MIRABELL. I am of another opinion. The greater the coxcomb, always the more the scandal; for a woman who is not a fool can have but one reason for associating with a man that is.

FAINALL. Are you jealous as often as you see Witwoud entertained by Millamant?

MIRABELL. Of her understanding I am, if not of her person.

FAINALL. You do her wrong; for to give her her due, she has wit.

MIRABELL. She has beauty enough to make any man think so, and complaisance enough not to contradict him who shall tell her so.

FAINALL. For a passionate lover, methinks you are a man somewhat too discerning in the failings of your mistress.

MIRABELL. And for a discerning man, somewhat too passionate a lover; for I like her with all her faults; nay, like her for her faults. Her follies are so natural, or so artful, that they become her; and those affectations which in another woman would be odious, serve but to make her more agreeable. I'll tell thee, Fainall, she once used me with that insolence, that in revenge I took her to pieces; sifted her, and separated her failings; I studied 'em, and got 'em by rote. The catalogue was so large that I was not without hopes one day or other to hate her heartily: to which end I so used myself to think of 'em that at length, contrary to my design and expectation, they gave me every hour less and less disturbance, till in a few days it became habitual to me to remember 'em without being displeased. They are now grown as familiar to me as my own frailties; and in all probability, in a little time longer I shall like 'em as well.

FAINALL. Marry her, marry her. Be half as well acquainted with her charms as you are with her defects, and my life on't, you are your own man again.

MIRABELL. Say you so?

FAINALL. Ay, ay, I have experience; I have a wife, and so forth.

Enter MESSENGER.

MESSENGER. Is one Squire Witwoud here?

BETTY. Yes; what's your business?

MESSENGER. I have a letter for him, from his brother Sir Wilfull, which I am charged to deliver into his own hands.

BETTY. He's in the next room, friend; that way.

Exit MESSENGER.

MIRABELL. What, is the chief of that noble family in town, Sir Wilfull Witwoud?

FAINALL. He is expected today. Do you know him?

MIRABELL. I have seen him. He promises to be an extraordinary person; I think you have the honour to be related to him.

FAINALL. Yes; he is half-brother to this Witwoud by a former wife, who was sister to my Lady Wishfort, my wife's mother. If you marry Millamant, you must call cousins too.

MIRABELL. I had rather be his relation than his acquaintance.

FAINALL. He comes to town in order to equip himself for travel.

MIRABELL. For travel! Why, the man that I mean is above forty!

FAINALL. No matter for that; 'tis for the honour of England that all Europe should know we have blockheads of all ages.

MIRABELL. I wonder there is not an act of parliament to save the credit of the nation and prohibit the exportation of fools.

FAINALL. By no means, 'tis better as 'tis. 'Tis better to trade with a little loss, than to be quite eaten up with being overstocked.

MIRABELL. Pray, are the follies of this knight errant and those of the squire his brother anything related?

FAINALL. Not at all; Witwoud grows by the knight like a medlar grafted on a crab. One will melt in your mouth, and t'other set your teeth on edge; one is all pulp, and the other all core.

MIRABELL. So one will be rotten before he be ripe, and the other will be rotten without ever being ripe at all.

FAINALL. Sir Wilfull is an odd mixture of bashfulness and obstinacy. But when he's drunk, he's as loving as the monster in *The Tempest*, and much after the same manner. To give t'other his due, he has something of good nature, and does not always want wit.

MIRABELL. Not always; but as often as his memory fails him, and his commonplace of comparisons. He is a fool with a good memory and some few scraps of other folks' wit. He is one whose conversation can never be approved, yet it is now and then to be endured. He has indeed one good quality, he is not exceptious; for he so passionately affects the reputation of understanding raillery, that he will construe an affront into a jest, and call downright rudeness and ill language, satire and fire.

FAINALL. If you have a mind to finish his picture, you have an opportunity to do it at full length. Behold the original!

Enter WITWOUD.

WITWOUD. Afford me your compassion, my dears! Pity me, Fainall, Mirabell, pity me!

MIRABELL. I do, from my soul.

FAINALL. Why, what's the matter?

WITWOUD. No letters for me, Betty?

BETTY. Did not the messenger bring you one but now, sir?

WITWOUD. Ay, but no other?

BETTY. No, sir.

WITWOUD. That's hard, that's very hard. A messenger, a mule, a beast of burden, he has brought me a letter from the fool my brother, as heavy as a panegyric in a funeral sermon, or a copy of commendatory verses from one poet to another. And what's worse, 'tis as sure a forerunner of the author as an epistle dedicatory.

MIRABELL. A fool, and your brother, Witwoud!

WITWOUD. Ay, ay, my half-brother. My half-brother he is, no nearer, upon honour.

MIRABELL. Then 'tis possible he may be but half a fool.

WITWOUD. Good, good, Mirabell *le drôle*! Good, good, hang him, don't let's talk of him. Fainall, how does your lady? Gad, I say anything in the world to get this fellow out of my head. I beg pardon that I should ask a man of pleasure and the town, a question at once so foreign and domestic. But I talk like an old maid at a marriage, I don't know what I say; but she's the best woman in the world.

FAINALL. 'Tis well you don t know what you say, or else your commendation would go near to make me either vain or jealous.

WITWOUD. No man in town lives well with a wife but Fainall. Your judgment, Mirabell?

MIRABELL. You had better step and ask his wife if you would be credibly informed.

WITWOUD. Mirabell.

MIRABELL. Ay.

WITWOUD. My dear, I ask ten thousand pardons. Gad, I have forgot what I was going to say to you.

MIRABELL. I thank you heartily, heartily.

WITWOUD. No, but prithee excuse me; my memory is such a memory.

MIRABELL. Have a care of such apologies, Witwoud; for I never knew a fool but he affected to complain either of the spleen or his memory.

FAINALL. What have you done with Petulant?

WITWOUD. He's reckoning his money – my money it was. I have no luck today.

FAINALL. You may allow him to win of you at play, for you are sure to be too hard for him at repartee; since you monopolise the wit that is between you, the fortune must be his of course.

MIRABELL. I don't find that Petulant confesses the superiority of wit to be your talent, Witwoud.

WITWOUD. Come, come, you are malicious now, and would breed debates. Petulant's my friend, and a very honest fellow, and a very pretty fellow, and has a smattering – faith and troth, a pretty deal of an odd sort of a small wit. Nay, I'll do him justice. I'm his friend, I won't wrong him neither. And if he had but any judgment in the world, he would not be altogether contemptible. Come come, don't detract from the merits of my friend.

FAINALL. You don't take your friend to be over-nicely bred?

WITWOUD. No, no, hang him, the rogue has no manners at all, that I must own. No more breeding than a bumbaily, that I grant you. 'Tis pity, faith; the fellow has fire and life.

MIRABELL. What, courage?

WITWOUD. Hum, faith, I don't know as to that; I can't say as to that. Yes, faith, in a controversy he'll contradict anybody.

MIRABELL. Though 'twere a man whom he feared, or a woman whom he loved.

WITWOUD. Well, well, he does not always think before he speaks; we have all our failings. You are too hard upon him, you are, faith. Let me excuse him; I can defend most of his faults, except one or two. One he has, that's the truth on't, if he were my brother, I could not acquit him. That, indeed, I could wish were otherwise.

MIRABELL. Ay, marry, what's that, Witwoud?

WITWOUD. O, pardon me. Expose the infirmities of my friend? No, my dear, excuse me there.

FAINALL. What, I warrant he's unsincere, or 'tis some such trifle.

WITWOUD. No, no, what if he be? 'Tis no matter for that; his wit will excuse that. A wit should no more be sincere than a woman constant. One argues a decay of parts, as t'other of beauty.

MIRABELL. Maybe you think him too positive?

WITWOUD. No, no, his being positive is an incentive to argument, and keeps up conversation.

FAINALL. Too illiterate?

WITWOUD. That! that's his happiness. His want of learning gives him the more opportunities to show his natural parts.

MIRABELL. He wants words.

WITWOUD. Ay, but I like him for that now; for his want of words gives me the pleasure very often to explain his meaning.

FAINALL. He s impudent.

WITWOUD. No; that's not it.

MIRABELL. Vain.

WITWOUD. No.

MIRABELL. What, he speaks unseasonable truths sometimes, because he has not wit enough to invent an evasion?

WITWOUD. Truths! Ha, ha, ha! No, no, since you will have it, I mean he never speaks truth at all, that's all. He will lie like a chambermaid, or a woman of quality's porter. Now that is a fault.

Enter a COACHMAN.

COACHMAN. Is Master Petulant here, mistress?

BETTY. Yes.

COACHMAN. Three gentlewomen in the coach would speak with him.

FAINALL. O brave Petulant; three!

BETTY. I'll tell him.

COACHMAN. You must bring two dishes of chocolate and a glass of cinnamon water.

Exit BETTY *and* COACHMAN.

WITWOUD. That should be for two fasting strumpets, and a bawd troubled with wind. Now you may know what the three are.

MIRABELL. You are very free with your friend's acquaintance.

WITWOUD. Ay, ay, friendship without freedom is as dull as love without enjoyment, or wine without toasting. But to tell you a secret, these are trulls that he allows coach-hire, and something more, by the week, to call on him once a day at public places.

MIRABELL. How!

WITWOUD. You shall see he won't go to 'em because there's no more company here to take notice of him. Why this is nothing to what he used to do; before he found out this way, I have known him call for himself.

FAINALL. Call for himself? What dost thou mean?

WITWOUD. Mean, why he would slip you out of this chocolate-house, just when you had been talking to him; as soon as your back was turned – whip, he was gone. Then trip to his lodging, clap on a hood and scarf and mask, slap into a hackney-coach, and drive hither to the door again in a trice, where he would send in for himself, that I mean, call for himself, wait for himself, nay, and what's more, not finding himself, sometimes leave a letter for himself.

MIRABELL. I confess this is something extraordinary. I believe he waits for himself now, he is so long a-coming. Oh, I ask his pardon.

Enter PETULANT.

BETTY. Sir, the coach stays.

PETULANT. Well, well, I come. 'Sbud, a man had as good be a
professed midwife as a professed whoremaster at this rate! To
be knocked up and raised at all hours, and in all places. Pox on
'em, I won't come. D'ye hear, tell 'em I won't come. Let 'em
snivel and cry their hearts out.

FAINALL. You are very cruel, Petulant.

PETULANT. All's one, let it pass. I have a humour to be cruel.

MIRABELL. I hope they are not persons of condition that you use
at this rate.

PETULANT. Condition? Condition's a dried fig, if I am not in
humour. By this hand, if they were your – a – a – your
what-d'ye-call-'ems themselves, they must wait or rub off, if
I want appetite.

MIRABELL. What-d'ye-call-'ems! What are they, Witwoud?

WITWOUD. Empresses, my dear; by your what-d'ye-call-'ems he
means Sultana queens.

PETULANT. Ay, Roxolanas.

MIRABELL. Cry you mercy.

FAINALL. Witwoud says they are

PETULANT. What does he say th'are?

WITWOUD. I? Fine ladies, I say.

PETULANT. Pass on, Witwoud. Harkee, by this light his relations:
two co-heiresses his cousins, and an old aunt that loves
caterwauling better than a conventicle.

WITWOUD. Ha, ha, ha! I had a mind to see how the rogue
would come off. Ha, ha, ha! Gad, I can't be angry with him, if
he said they were my mother and my sisters.

MIRABELL. No!

WITWOUD. No; the rogue's wit and readiness of invention charm
me; dear Petulant!

BETTY. They are gone, sir, in great anger.

PETULANT. Enough, let 'em trundle. Anger helps complexion, saves paint.

FAINALL. This continence is all dissembled; this is in order to have something to brag of the next time he makes court to Millamant, and swear he has abandoned the whole sex for her sake.

MIRABELL. Have you not left your impudent pretensions there yet? I shall cut your throat sometime or other, Petulant, about that business.

PETULANT. Ay, ay, let that pass. There are other throats to be cut –

MIRABELL. Meaning mine, sir?

PETULANT. Not I – I mean nobody – I know nothing. But there are uncles and nephews in the world, and they may be rivals – what then? All's one for that.

MIRABELL. How! Harkee Petulant, come hither. Explain, or I shall call your interpreter.

PETULANT. Explain? I know nothing. Why, you have an uncle, have you not, lately come to town, and lodges by my Lady Wishfort's?

MIRABELL. True.

PETULANT. Why, that's enough. You and he are not friends; and if he should marry and have a child, you may be disinherited, ha?

MIRABELL. Where hast thou stumbled upon all this truth?

PETULANT. All's one for that. Why then, say I know something.

MIRABELL. Come, thou art an honest fellow, Petulant, and shalt make love to my mistress, thou shalt, i'faith. What hast thou heard of my uncle?

PETULANT. I? Nothing I. If throats are to be cut, let swords clash. Snug's the word; I shrug and am silent.

MIRABELL. O raillery, raillery. Come, I know thou art in the women's secrets. What, you're a cabalist; I know you stayed at Millamant's last night, after I went. Was there any mention made of my uncle, or me? Tell me. If thou hadst but good nature equal to thy wit, Petulant, Tony Witwoud, who is now thy competitor in fame, would show as dim by thee as a dead whiting's eye by a pearl of orient. He would no more be seen by thee than Mercury is by the sun. Come, I'm sure thou wilt tell me.

PETULANT. If I do, will you grant me common sense then, for the future?

MIRABELL. Faith, I'll do what I can for thee; and I'll pray that heaven may grant it thee in the meantime.

PETULANT. Well, harkee .

MIRABELL *and* PETULANT *talk apart.*

FAINALL. Petulant and you both will find Mirabell as warm a rival as a lover.

WITWOUD. Pshaw! pshaw! That she laughs at Petulant is plain. And for my part, but that it is almost a fashion to admire her, I should. Harkee, to tell you a secret, but let it go no further – between friends, I shall never break my heart for her.

FAINALL. How!

WITWOUD. She's handsome; but she's a sort of an uncertain woman.

FAINALL. I thought you had died for her.

WITWOUD. Umh – no –

FAINALL. She has wit.

WITWOUD. 'Tis what she will hardly allow anybody else. Now, demme, I should hate that, if she were as handsome as Cleopatra. Mirabell is not so sure of her as he thinks for.

FAINALL. Why do you think so?

WITWOUD. We stayed pretty late there last night, and heard something of an uncle to Mirabell, who is lately come to town, and is between him and the best part of his estate. Mirabell and he are at some distance, as my Lady Wishfort has been told; and you know she hates Mirabell worse than a Quaker hates a parrot, or than a fishmonger hates a hard frost. Whether this uncle has seen Mrs Millamant or not, I cannot say; but there were items of such a treaty being in embryo, and if it should come to life, poor Mirabell would be in some sort unfortunately fobbed, i'faith.

FAINALL. 'Tis impossible Millamant should hearken to it.

WITWOUD. Faith, my dear, I can't tell; she's a woman, and a kind of a humorist.

MIRABELL. And this is the sum of what you could collect last night?

PETULANT. The quintessence. Maybe Witwoud knows more; he stayed longer. Besides, they never mind him; they say anything before him.

MIRABELL. I thought you had been the greatest favourite.

PETULANT. Ay, *tête à tête*, but not in public, because I make remarks.

MIRABELL. Do you?

PETULANT. Ay, ay, pox, I'm malicious, man. Now he's soft you know; they are not in awe of him. The fellow's well-bred; he's what you call a – what-d'ye-call-'em – a fine gentleman; but he's silly withal.

MIRABELL. I thank you, I know as much as my curiosity requires. Fainall, are you for the Mall?

FAINALL. Ay, I'll take a turn before dinner.

WITWOUD. Ay, we'll all walk in the park; the ladies talked of being there.

MIRABELL. l thought you were obliged to watch for your brother Sir Wilfull's arrival.

WITWOUD. No, no, he comes to his aunt's, my Lady Wishfort.
Pox on him, I shall be troubled with him too; what shall I do
with the fool?

PETULANT. Beg him for his estate, that I may beg you afterwards, and so have but one trouble with you both.

WITWOUD. O rare Petulant! Thou art as quick as a fire in a
frosty morning; thou shalt to the Mall with us, and we'll be
very severe.

PETULANT. Enough. I'm in a humour to be severe.

MIRABELL. Are you? Pray then walk by yourselves – let not us
be accessory to your putting the ladies out of countenance with
your senseless ribaldry, which you roar out aloud as often as
they pass by you; and when you have made a handsome
woman blush, then you think you have been severe.

PETULANT. What, what? Then let 'em either show their
innocence by not understanding what they hear, or else show
their discretion by not hearing what they would not be thought
to understand.

MIRABELL. But hast not thou then sense enough to know that
thou ought'st to be most ashamed thyself, when thou hast put
another out of countenance?

PETULANT. Not I, by this hand. I always take blushing either for
a sign of guilt, or ill breeding.

MIRABELL. I confess you ought to think so. You are in the right,
that you may plead the error of your judgment in defence of
your practice.

Where modesty's ill manners, 'tis but fit
That impudence and malice pass for wit.

Exeunt.

ACT TWO

Scene One

St James's Park.

Enter MRS FAINALL *and* MRS MARWOOD.

MRS FAINALL. Ay, ay, dear Marwood, if we will be happy, we must find the means in ourselves, and among ourselves. Men are ever in extremes, either doting or averse. While they are lovers, if they have fire and sense, their jealousies are insupportable; and when they cease to love (we ought to think at least) they loathe. They look upon us with horror and distaste; they meet us like the ghosts of what we were, and as such fly from us.

MRS MARWOOD. True, 'tis an unhappy circumstance of life, that love should ever die before us; and that the man so often should outlive the lover. But say what you will, 'tis better to be left than never to have been loved. To pass our youth in dull indifference, to refuse the sweets of life because they once must leave us, is as preposterous as to wish to have been born old, because we one day must be old. For my part, my youth may wear and waste, but it shall never rust in my possession.

MRS FAINALL. Then it seems you dissemble an aversion to mankind, only in compliance with my mother's humour.

MRS MARWOOD. Certainly. To be free, I have no taste of those insipid dry discourses with which our sex of force must entertain themselves apart from men. We may affect endearments to each other, profess eternal friendships, and seem to dote like lovers; but 'tis not in our natures long to persevere. Love will resume his empire in our breasts, and every heart, or soon or late, receive and readmit him as its lawful tyrant.

MRS FAINALL. Bless me, how have I been deceived! Why, you profess a libertine!

MRS MARWOOD. You see my friendship by my freedom. Come, be as sincere, acknowledge that your sentiments agree with mine.

MRS FAINALL. Never.

MRS MARWOOD. You hate mankind?

MRS FAINALL. Heartily, inveterately.

MRS MARWOOD. Your husband?

MRS FAINALL. Most transcendently. Ay, though I say it, meritoriously.

MRS MARWOOD. Give me your hand upon it.

MRS FAINALL. There.

MRS MARWOOD. I join with you; what I have said has been to try you.

MRS FAINALL. Is it possible? Dost thou hate those vipers, men?

MRS MARWOOD. I have done hating em, and am now come to despise 'em; the next thing I have to do, is eternally to forget 'em.

MRS FAINALL. There spoke the spirit of an Amazon, a Penthesilea.

MRS MARWOOD. And yet I am thinking sometimes to carry my aversion further.

MRS FAINALL. How?

MRS MARWOOD. Faith, by marrying; if I could but find one that loved me very well and would be thoroughly sensible of ill usage, I think I should do myself the violence of undergoing the ceremony.

MRS FAINALL. You would not make him a cuckold?

MRS MARWOOD. No; but I'd make him believe I did, and that's as bad.

MRS FAINALL. Why, had not you as good do it?

MRS MARWOOD. Oh, if he should ever discover it, he would then know the worst, and be out of his pain; but I would have him ever to continue upon the rack of fear and jealousy.

MRS FAINALL. Ingenious mischief! Would thou wert married to Mirabell.

MRS MARWOOD. Would I were.

MRS FAINALL. You change colour.

MRS MARWOOD. Because I hate him.

MRS FAINALL. So do I; but I can hear him named. But what reason have you to hate him in particular?

MRS MARWOOD. I never loved him; he is, and always was, insufferably proud.

MRS FAINALL. By the reason you give for your aversion, one would think it dissembled; for you have laid a fault to his charge of which his enemies must acquit him.

MRS MARWOOD. Oh, then it seems you are one of his favourable enemies. Methinks you look a little pale, and now you flush again.

MRS FAINALL. Do I? I think I am a little sick o' the sudden.

MRS MARWOOD. What ails you?

MRS FAINALL. My husband. Don't you see him? He turned short upon me unawares, and has almost overcome me.

Enter FAINALL *and* MIRABELL.

MRS MARWOOD. Ha, ha, ha; he comes opportunely for you.

MRS FAINALL. For you, for he has brought Mirabell with him.

FAINALL. My dear.

MRS FAINALL. My soul.

FAINALL. You don't look well today, child.

MRS FAINALL. D'ye think so?

MIRABELL. He is the only man that does, madam.

MRS FAINALL. The only man that would tell me so at least; and the only man from whom I could hear it without mortification.

FAINALL. Oh, my dear, I am satisfied of your tenderness; I know you cannot resent anything from me; especially what is an effect of my concern.

MRS FAINALL. Mr Mirabell, my mother interrupted you in a pleasant relation last night; I would fain hear it out.

MIRABELL. The persons concerned in that affair have yet a tolerable reputation; I am afraid Mr Fainall will be censorious.

MRS FAINALL. He has a humour more prevailing than his curiosity and will willingly dispense with the hearing of one scandalous story, to avoid giving an occasion to make another by being seen to walk with his wife. This way Mr Mirabell, and I dare promise you will oblige us both.

Exeunt MRS FAINALL *and* MIRABELL.

FAINALL. Excellent creature! Well sure if I should live to be rid of my wife, I should be a miserable man.

MRS MARWOOD. Ay!

FAINALL. For having only that one hope, the accomplishment of it, of consequence, must put an end to all my hopes; and what a wretch is he who must survive his hopes! Nothing remains when that day comes, but to sit down and weep like Alexander, when he wanted other worlds to conquer.

MRS MARWOOD. Will you not follow 'em?

FAINALL. Faith, I think not.

MRS MARWOOD. Pray let us; I have a reason.

FAINALL. You are not jealous?

MRS MARWOOD. Of whom?

FAINALL. Of Mirabell.

MRS MARWOOD. If I am, is it inconsistent with my love to you that I am tender of your honour?

FAINALL. You would intimate then, as if there were a fellow-feeling between my wife and him.

MRS MARWOOD. I think she does not hate him to that degree she would be thought.

FAINALL. But he, I fear, is too insensible.

MRS MARWOOD. It may be you are deceived.

FAINALL. It may be so. I do now begin to apprehend it.

MRS MARWOOD. What?

FAINALL. That I have been deceived madam, and you are false.

MRS MARWOOD. That I am false! What mean you?

FAINALL. To let you know I see through all your little arts. Come, you both love him, and both have equally dissembled your aversion. Your mutual jealousies of one another have made you clash till you have both struck fire. I have seen the warm confession reddening on your cheeks and sparkling from your eyes.

MRS MARWOOD. You do me wrong.

FAINALL. I do not. 'Twas for my ease to oversee and wilfully neglect the gross advances made him by my wife; that by permitting her to be engaged, I might continue unsuspected in my pleasures, and take you oftener to my arms in full security. But could you think, because the nodding husband would not wake, that e'er the watchful lover slept?

MRS MARWOOD. And wherewithal can you reproach me?

FAINALL. With infidelity, with loving of another, with love of Mirabell.

MRS MARWOOD. 'Tis false. I challenge you to show an instance that can confirm your groundless accusation. I hate him.

FAINALL. And wherefore do you hate him? He is insensible, and your resentment follows his neglect. An instance? The injuries you have done him are a proof: your interposing in his love. What cause had you to make discoveries of his pretended passion? To undeceive the credulous aunt, and be the officious obstacle of his match with Millamant?

MRS MARWOOD. My obligations to my lady urged me. I had professed a friendship to her, and could not see her easy nature so abused by that dissembler.

FAINALL. What, was it conscience then? Professed a friendship! Oh the pious friendships of the female sex!

MRS MARWOOD. More tender, more sincere, and more enduring than all the vain and empty vows of men, whether professing love to us, or mutual faith to one another.

FAINALL. Ha, ha, ha! You are my wife's friend too.

MRS MARWOOD. Shame and ingratitude! Do you reproach me? You, you upbraid me! Have I been false to her through strict fidelity to you, and sacrificed my friendship to keep my love inviolate? And have you the baseness to charge me with the guilts unmindful of the merit! To you it should be meritorious that I have been vicious. And do you reflect that guilt upon me, which should lie buried in your bosom?

FAINALL. You misinterpret my reproof. I meant but to remind you of the slight account you once could make of strictest ties, when set in competition with your love to me.

MRS MARWOOD. 'Tis false, you urged it with deliberate malice. 'Twas spoke in scorn, and I never will forgive it.

FAINALL. Your guilt, not your resentment, begets your rage. If yet you loved, you could forgive a jealousy; but you are stung to find you are discovered.

MRS MARWOOD. It shall be all discovered. You too shall be discovered. Be sure you shall. I can but be exposed. If I do it myself, I shall prevent your baseness.

FAINALL. Why, what will you do?

MRS MARWOOD. Disclose it to your wife; own what has passed between us.

FAINALL. Frenzy!

MRS MARWOOD. By all my wrongs I'll do't. I'll publish to the world the injuries you have done me, both in my fame and fortune. With both I trusted you, you bankrupt in honour, as indigent of wealth.

FAINALL. Your fame I have preserved. Your fortune has been bestowed as the prodigality of your love would have it, in pleasures which we both have shared. Yet had not you been false, I had ere this repaid it. 'Tis true! Had you permitted Mirabell with Millamant to have stolen their marriage, my lady had been incensed beyond all means of reconcilement; Millamant had forfeited the moiety of her fortune, which then would have descended to my wife. And wherefore did I marry, but to make lawful prize of a rich widow's wealth, and squander it on love and you?

MRS MARWOOD. Deceit and frivolous pretence.

FAINALL. Death, am I not married? What's pretence? Am I not imprisoned, fettered? Have I not a wife? Nay a wife that was a widow, a young widow, a handsome widow; and would be again a widow, but that I have a heart of proof, and something of a constitution to bustle through the ways of wedlock and this world. Will you yet be reconciled to truth and me?

MRS MARWOOD. Impossible. Truth and you are inconsistent. I hate you, and shall for ever.

FAINALL. For loving you?

MRS MARWOOD. I loathe the name of love after such usage; and next to the guilt with which you would asperse me, I scorn you most. Farewell.

FAINALL. Nay, we must not part thus.

MRS MARWOOD. Let me go.

FAINALL. Come, I'm sorry.

MRS MARWOOD. I care not, let me go. Break my hands, do!
I'd leave 'em to get loose.

FAINALL. I would not hurt you for the world. Have I no other
hold to keep you here?

MRS MARWOOD. Well, I have deserved it all.

FAINALL. You know I love you.

MRS MARWOOD. Poor dissembling! Oh, that – well, it is not
yet –

FAINALL. What? What is it not? What is it not yet? It is not yet
too late

MRS MARWOOD. No, it is not yet too late – I have that
comfort.

FAINALL. It is, to love another.

MRS MARWOOD. But not to loathe, detest, abhor mankind,
myself, and the whole treacherous world.

FAINALL. Nay, this is extravagance. Come, I ask your pardon.
No tears. I was to blame; I could not love you and be easy in
my doubts. Pray, forbear. I believe you; I'm convinced I've
done you wrong, and any way, every way, will make amends.
I'll hate my wife yet more, damn her. I'll part with her, rob her
of all she's worth, and we'll retire somewhere, anywhere, to
another world. I'll marry thee; be pacified. 'Sdeath, they come;
hide your face, your tears. You have a mask; wear it a moment.
This way, this way. Be persuaded.

Exeunt.

Enter MIRABELL *and* MRS FAINALL.

MRS FAINALL. They are here yet.

MIRABELL. They are turning into the other walk.

MRS FAINALL. While I only hated my husband, I could bear to
see him; but since I have despised him, he's too offensive.

MIRABELL. Oh, you should hate with prudence.

MRS FAINALL. Yes, for I have loved with indiscretion.

MIRABELL. You should have just so much disgust for your husband as may be sufficient to make you relish your lover.

MRS FAINALL. You have been the cause that I have loved without bounds, and would you set limits to that aversion of which you have been the occasion? Why did you make me marry this man?

MIRABELL. Why do we daily commit disagreeable and dangerous actions? To save that idol, reputation. If the familiarities of our loves had produced that consequence of which you were apprehensive, where could you have fixed a father's name with credit, but on a husband? I knew Fainall to be a man lavish of his morals, an interested and professing friend, a false and a designing lover; yet one whose wit and outward fair behaviour have gained a reputation with the town enough to make that woman stand excused who has suffered herself to be won by his addresses. A better man ought not to have been sacrificed to the occasion; a worse had not answered to the purpose. When you are weary of him, you know your remedy.

MRS FAINALL. I ought to stand in some degree of credit with you, Mirabell.

MIRABELL. In justice to you, I have made you privy to my whole design, and put it in your power to ruin or advance my fortune.

MRS FAINALL. Whom have you instructed to represent your pretended uncle?

MIRABELL. Waitwell, my servant.

MRS FAINALL. He is an humble servant to Foible, my mother's woman, and may win her to your interest.

MIRABELL. Care is taken for that – she is won and worn by this time. They were married this morning.

MRS FAINALL. Who?

MIRABELL. Waitwell and Foible. I would not tempt my servant to betray me by trusting him too far. If your mother, in hopes to ruin me, should consent to marry my pretended uncle, he might, like Mosca in *The Fox*, stand upon terms; so I made him sure beforehand.

MRS FAINALL. So, if my poor mother is caught in a contract, you will discover the imposture betimes, and release her by producing a certificate of her gallant's former marriage.

MIRABELL. Yes, upon condition she consent to my marriage with her niece, and surrender the moiety of her fortune in her possession.

MRS FAINALL. She talked last night of endeavouring at a match between Millamant and your uncle.

MIRABELL. That was by Foible's direction, and my instruction, that she might seem to carry it more privately.

MRS FAINALL. Well, I have an opinion of your success, for I believe my lady will do anything to get a husband; and when she has this, which you have provided for her, I suppose she will submit to anything to get rid of him.

MIRABELL. Yes, I think the good lady would marry anything that resembled a man, though 'twere no more than what a butler could pinch out of a napkin.

MRS FAINALL. Female frailty! We must all come to it, if we live to be old, and feel the craving of a false appetite when the true is decayed.

MIRABELL. An old woman's appetite is depraved like that of a girl. 'Tis the green sickness of a second childhood, and, like the faint offer of a latter spring, serves but to usher in the fall, and withers in an affected bloom.

MRS FAINALL. Here's your mistress.

Enter MRS MILLAMANT, WITWOUD, *and* MINCING.

MIRABELL. Here she comes, i'faith, full sail, with her fan spread and her streamers out, and a shoal of fools for tenders. Ha, no, I cry her mercy.

MRS FAINALL. I see but one poor empty sculler, and he tows her woman after him.

MIRABELL. You seem to be unattended, madam. You used to have the *beau monde* throng after you, and a flock of gay, fine perukes hovering round you.

WITWOUD. Like moths about a candle. I had like to have lost my comparison for want of breath.

MILLAMANT. Oh, I have denied myself airs today. I have walked as I fast through the crowd –

WITWOUD. As a favourite in disgrace; and with as few followers.

MILLAMANT. Dear Mr Witwoud, truce with your similitudes; for I am as sick of 'em –

WITWOUD. As a physician of a good air. I cannot help it madam, though 'tis against myself.

MILLAMANT. Yet again! Mincing, stand between me and his wit.

WITWOUD. Do, Mrs Mincing, like a screen before a great fire. I confess I do blaze today; I am too bright.

MRS FAINALL. But dear Millamant, why were you so long?

MILLAMANT. Long! Lord, have I not made violent haste? I have asked every living thing I met for you; I have enquired after you as after a new fashion.

WITWOUD. Madam, truce with your similitudes. No, you met her husband, and did not ask him for her.

MIRABELL. By your leave, Witwoud, that were like enquiring after an old fashion, to ask a husband for his wife.

WITWOUD. Hum; a hit, a hit, a palpable hit, I confess it.

MRS FAINALL. You were dressed before I came abroad.

MILLAMANT. Ay, that's true. Oh, but then I had – Mincing, what had I? Why was I so long?

MINCING. Oh mem, your la'ship stayed to peruse a pecquet of letters.

MILLAMANT. Oh, ay, letters – I had letters – I am persecuted with letters – I hate letters. Nobody knows how to write letters; and yet one has 'em, one does not know why. They serve one to pin up one's hair.

WITWOUD. Is that the way? Pray madam, do you pin up your hair with all your letters? I find I must keep copies.

MILLAMANT. Only with those in verse, Mr Witwoud. I never pin up my hair with prose. I fancy one's hair would not curl if it were pinned up with prose. I think I tried once, Mincing.

MINCING. Oh mem, I shall never forget it.

MILLAMANT. Ay, poor Mincing tift and tift all the morning.

MINCING. Till I had the cremp in my fingers I'll vow, mem. And all to no purpose. But when your la'ship pins it up with poetry, it sits so pleasant the next day as anything, and is so pure and so crips.

WITWOUD. Indeed, so crips?

MINCING. You're such a critic Mr Witwoud.

MILLAMANT. Mirabell, did not you take exceptions last night? Oh, ay, and went away. Now I think on't, I'm angry. No, now I think on't I'm pleased, for I believe I gave you some pain.

MIRABELL. Does that please you?

MILLAMANT. Infinitely; I love to give pain.

MIRABELL. You would affect a cruelty which is not in your nature; your true vanity is in the power of pleasing.

MILLAMANT. Oh, I ask your pardon for that. One's cruelty is one's power, and when one parts with one's cruelty, one parts with one's power; and when one has parted with that, I fancy one's old and ugly.

MIRABELL. Ay, ay, suffer your cruelty to ruin the object of your power, to destroy your lover and then how vain, how lost a thing you'll be! Nay, 'tis true: you are no longer handsome when you've lost your lover; your beauty dies upon the instant.

For beauty is the lover's gift; 'tis he bestows your charms, your glass is all a cheat. The ugly and the old, whom the looking-glass mortifies, yet after commendation can be flattered by it, and discover beauties in it; for that reflects our praises, rather than your face.

MILLAMANT. Oh, the vanity of these men! Fainall, d'ye hear him? If they did not commend us, we were not handsome! Now you must know they could not commend one, if one was not handsome. Beauty the lover's gift – Lord, what is a lover, that it can give? Why, one makes lovers as fast as one pleases, and they live as long as one pleases, and they die as soon as one pleases; and then, if one pleases, one makes more.

WITWOUD. Very pretty. Why, you make no more of making of lovers, madam, than of making so many card-matches.

MILLAMANT. One no more owes one's beauty to a lover, than one's wit to an echo. They can but reflect what we look and say; vain empty things if we are silent or unseen, and want a being.

MIRABELL. Yet to those two vain empty things you owe two of the greatest pleasures of your life.

MILLAMANT. How so?

MIRABELL. To your lover you owe the pleasure of hearing yourselves praised; and to an echo the pleasure of hearing yourselves talk.

WITWOUD. But I know a lady that loves talking so incessantly she won't give an echo fair play; she has that everlasting rotation of tongue, that an echo must wait till she dies before it can catch her last words.

MILLAMANT. Oh, fiction! Fainall, let us leave these men.

MIRABELL (*aside to* MRS FAINALL). Draw off Witwoud.

MRS FAINALL. Immediately. I have a word or two for Mr Witwoud.

MIRABELL. I would beg a little private audience too –

Exit WITWOUD *and* MRS FAINALL.

You had the tyranny to deny me last night, though you knew
I came to impart a secret to you that concerned my love.

MILLAMANT. You saw I was engaged.

MIRABELL. Unkind. You had the leisure to entertain a herd
of fools; things who visit you from their excessive idleness,
bestowing on your easiness that time which is the encumbrance
of their lives. How can you find delight in such society? It is
impossible they should admire you; they are not capable. Or
if they were, it should be to you as a mortification; for sure,
to please a fool is some degree of folly.

MILLAMANT. I please myself. Besides, sometimes to converse
with fools is for my health.

MIRABELL. Your health! Is there a worse disease than the
conversation of fools?

MILLAMANT. Yes, the vapours; fools are physics for it, next to
assafoetida.

MIRABELL. You are not in a course of fools?

MILLAMANT. Mirabell, if you persist in this offensive freedom
you'll displease me. I think I must resolve, after all, not to have
you; we shan't agree.

MIRABELL. Not in our physic, it may be.

MILLAMANT. And yet our distemper in all likelihood will be the
same; for we shall be sick of one another. I shan't endure to be
reprimanded, nor instructed; 'tis so dull to act always by advice,
and so tedious to be told of one's faults – I can't bear it. Well, I
won't have you Mirabell – I'm resolved – I think – you may go.
Ha, ha, ha! What would you give, that you could help loving me?

MIRABELL. I would give something that you did not know I
could not help it.

MILLAMANT. Come, don't look grave then. Well, what do you
say to me?

MIRABELL. I say that a man may as soon make a friend by his wit, or a fortune by his honesty, as win a woman with plain dealing and sincerity.

MILLAMANT. Sententious Mirabell! Prithee, don't look with that violent and inflexible wise face, like Solomon at the dividing of the child in an old tapestry hanging.

MIRABELL. You are merry, madam, but I would persuade you for one moment to be serious.

MILLAMANT. What, with that face? No, if you keep your countenance, 'tis impossible I should hold mine. Well, after all, there is something very moving in a lovesick face. Ha, ha, ha! Well, I won't laugh; don't be peevish. Heigho! Now I'll be melancholy, as melancholy as a watchlight. Well, Mirabell, if ever you will win me, woo me now. Nay, if you are so tedious, fare you well; I see they are walking away.

MIRABELL. Can you not find in the variety of your disposition one moment –

MILLAMANT. To hear you tell me that Foible's married, and your plot like to speed? No.

MIRABELL. But how came you to know it?

MILLAMANT. Unless by the help of the devil, you can't imagine; unless she should tell me herself. Which of the two it may have been, I will leave you to consider; and when you have done thinking of that, think of me.

Exit.

MIRABELL. I have something more – gone! Think of you? To think of a whirlwind, though 'twere in a whirlwind, were a case of more steady contemplation; a very tranquillity of mind and mansion. A fellow that lives in a windmill has not a more whimsical dwelling than the heart of a man that is lodged in a woman. There is no point of the compass to which they cannot turn, and by which they are not turned; and by one as well as another, for motion, not method is their occupation. To know this, and yet continue to be in love, is to be made wise from the dictates of reason, and yet persevere to play the fool by the force of instinct. Oh, here come my pair of turtles. What, billing so sweetly? Is not Valentine's day over with you yet?

Enter WAITWELL *and* FOIBLE.

Sirrah Waitwell, why sure you think you were married for your own recreation, and not for my conveniency.

WAITWELL. Your pardon, sir. With submission, we have indeed been solacing in lawful delights; but still with an eye to business, sir. I have instructed her as well as I could. If she can take your directions as readily as my instructions, sir, your affairs are in a prosperous way.

MIRABELL. Give you joy, Mrs Foible.

FOIBLE. Oh las, sir, I'm so ashamed. I'm afraid my lady has been in a thousand inquietudes for me. But I protest, sir, I made as much haste as I could.

WAITWELL. That she did indeed, sir. It was my fault that she did not make more.

MIRABELL. That I believe.

FOIBLE. But I told my lady as you instructed me, sir: that I had a prospect of seeing Sir Rowland your uncle, and that I would put her ladyship's picture in my pocket to show him; which I'll be sure to say has made him so enamoured of her beauty, that he burns with impatience to lie at her ladyship's feet and worship the original.

MIRABELL. Excellent Foible! Matrimony has made you eloquent in love.

WAITWELL. I think she has profited, sir. I think so.

FOIBLE. You have seen Madam Millamant, sir?

MIRABELL. Yes.

FOIBLE. I told her, sir, because I did not know that you might find an opportunity; she had so much company last night.

MIRABELL. Your diligence will merit more. In the meantime –

Gives money.

FOIBLE. Oh dear sir, your humble servant.

WAITWELL. Spouse.

MIRABELL. Stand off, sir, not a penny Go on and prosper, Foible; the lease shall be made good and the farm stocked, if we succeed.

FOIBLE. I don't question your generosity, sir; and you need not doubt of success. If you have no more commands, sir, I'll be gone; I'm sure my lady is at her toilet, and can't dress till I come. (*Looking out.*) Oh dear, I'm sure that was Mrs Marwood that went by in a mask; if she has seen me with you I'm sure she'll tell my lady. I'll make haste home and prevent her. Your servant, sir. B'w'y, Waitwell.

Exit FOIBLE.

WAITWELL. Sir Rowland, if you please. The jade's so pert upon her preferment she forgets herself.

MIRABELL. Come sir, will you endeavour to forget yourself, and transform into Sir Rowland?

WAITWELL. Why sir, it will be impossible I should remember myself. Married, knighted, and attended all in one day! 'Tis enough to make any man forget himself. The difficulty will be how to recover my acquaintance and familiarity with my former self, and fall from my transformation to a reformation into Waitwell. Nay, I shan't be quite the same Waitwell, neither – for now I remember me, I am married, and can't be my own man again.

Ay there's the grief; that's the sad change of life;
To lose my title, and yet keep my wife.

Exeunt.

ACT THREE

Scene One

A Room in Lady Wishfort's House.

LADY WISHFORT *at her toilet,* PEG *waiting.*

LADY WISHFORT. Merciful, no news of Foible yet?

PEG. No, madam.

LADY WISHFORT. I have no more patience. If I have not
fretted myself till I am pale again, there's no veracity in me.
Fetch me the red – the red, do you hear, sweetheart? An arrant
ash colour, as I'm a person. Look you how this wench stirs!
Why dost thou not fetch me a little red? Did'st thou not hear
me, Mopus?

PEG. The red ratafia does your ladyship mean, or the cherry
brandy?

LADY WISHFORT. Ratafia, fool? No, fool. Not the ratafia, fool –
grant me patience! I mean the Spanish paper, idiot; complexion,
darling. Paint, paint, paint; dost thou understand that, changeling, dangling thy hands like bobbins before thee? Why dost
thou not stir, puppet? Thou wooden thing upon wires!

PEG. Lord, madam, your ladyship is so impatient. I cannot come
at the paint, madam; Mrs Foible has locked it up, and carried
the key with her.

LADY WISHFORT. A pox take you both! Fetch me the cherry
brandy then. (*Exit* PEG.) I'm as pale and as faint, I look like
Mrs Qualmsick, the curate's wife, that's always breeding.
Wench, come, come, wench, what art thou doing? Sipping?
Tasting? Save thee, dost thou not know the bottle?

Enter PEG *with a bottle and china cup.*

PEG. Madam, I was looking for a cup.

LADY WISHFORT. A cup, save thee. And what a cup hast thou brought! Dost thou take me for a fairy, to drink out of an acorn? Why didst thou not bring thy thimble? Hast thou ne'er a brass thimble clinking in thy pocket with a bit of nutmeg? I warrant thee. Come, fill, fill. So – again. (*One knocks.*) See who that is. Set down the bottle first. Here, here, under the table. What, wouldst thou go with the bottle in thy hand like a tapster? As I'm a person, this wench has lived in an inn upon the road before she came to me, like Maritornes the Asturian in *Don Quixote*. No Foible yet?

PEG. No, madam; Mrs Marwood.

LADY WISHFORT. Oh, Marwood, let her come in. Come in, good Marwood.

Enter MRS MARWOOD.

MRS MARWOOD. I'm surprised to find your ladyship in *déshabille* at this time of day.

LADY WISHFORT. Foible's a lost thing; has been abroad since morning, and never heard of since.

MRS MARWOOD. I saw her but now, as I came masked through the park, in conference with Mirabell.

LADY WISHFORT. With Mirabell! You call my blood into my face with mentioning that traitor. She durst not have the confidence. I sent her to negotiate an affair in which if I'm detected I'm undone. If that wheedling villain has wrought upon Foible to detect me, I'm ruined. Oh my dear friend, I'm a wretch of wretches if I'm detected.

MRS MARWOOD. Oh madam, you cannot suspect Mrs Foible's integrity.

LADY WISHFORT. Oh, he carries poison in his tongue that would corrupt integrity itself. If she has given him an opportunity, she has as good as put her integrity into his hands. Ah, dear Marwood, what's integrity to an opportunity? Hark! I hear her. Go, you thing, and send her in. (*Exit* PEG.) Dear friend, retire into my closet, that I may examine her with more freedom. You'll pardon me, dear friend; I can make bold with you. There are books over the chimney – Quarles and Prynne, and the *Short View of the Stage*, with Bunyan's works, to entertain you.

Exit MARWOOD.

Enter FOIBLE.

O Foible, where hast thou been? What hast thou been doing?

FOIBLE. Madam, I have seen the party.

LADY WISHFORT. But what hast thou done?

FOIBLE. Nay, 'tis your ladyship has done, and are to do; I have only promised. But a man so enamoured – so transported! Well, here it is, all that is left; all that is not kissed away. Well, if worshipping of pictures be a sin, poor Sir Rowland, I say.

LADY WISHFORT. The miniature has been counted like. But hast thou not betrayed me, Foible? Hast thou not detected me to that faithless Mirabell? What hadst thou to do with him in the park? Answer me, he has got nothing out of thee?

FOIBLE (*aside*). So, the devil has been beforehand with me. What shall I say? Alas, madam, could I help it, if I met that confident thing? Was I in fault? If you had heard how he used me, and all upon your ladyship's account, I'm sure you would not suspect my fidelity. Nay, if that had been the worst, I could have borne; but he had a fling at your ladyship too, and then I could not hold, but i'faith I gave him his own.

LADY WISHFORT. Me? What did the filthy fellow say?

FOIBLE. Oh madam, 'tis a shame to say what he said, with his taunts and his fleers, tossing up his nose. 'Humh!' says he, 'what, you are ahatching some plot,' says he, 'you are so early abroad, or catering,' says he, 'ferreting for some disbanded officer, I warrant. Half-pay is but thin subsistence,' says he. 'Well, what pension does your lady propose? Let me see,' says he. 'What, she must come down pretty deep, now she's superannuated,' says he, 'and – '

LADY WISHFORT. Ods my life, I'll have him, I'll have him murdered. I'll have him poisoned. Where does he eat? I'll marry a drawer to have him poisoned in his wine. I'll send for Robin from Locket's immediately.

FOIBLE. Poison him? Poisoning's too good for him. Starve him madam, starve him; marry Sir Rowland and get him disinherited. Oh, you would bless yourself to hear what he said.

LADY WISHFORT. A villain! Superannuated!

FOIBLE. 'Humh,' says he, 'I hear you are laying designs against me too,' says he, 'and Mrs Millamant is to marry my uncle' (he does not suspect a word of your ladyship); 'but,' says he, 'I'll fit you for that, I warrant you,' says he. 'I'll hamper you for that,' says he, 'you and your old frippery too,' says he, 'I'll handle you – '

LADY WISHFORT. Audacious villain! 'handle' me, would he durst! 'Frippery? Old frippery!' Was there ever such a foul-mouthed fellow? I'll be married tomorrow, I'll be contracted tonight!

FOIBLE. The sooner the better madam.

LADY WISHFORT. Will Sir Rowland be here, sayest thou? When, Foible?

FOIBLE. Incontinently, madam. No new sheriff's wife expects the return of her husband after knighthood with that impatience in which Sir Rowland burns for the dear hour of kissing your ladyship's hands after dinner.

LADY WISHFORT. 'Frippery! Superannuated frippery!' I'll frippery the villain; I'll reduce him to frippery and rags! A tatterdemalion! I hope to see him hung with tatters, like a Long Lane penthouse or a gibbet thief. A slander-mouthed railer. I warrant the spendthrift prodigal's in debt as much as the million lottery, or the whole court upon a birthday. I'll spoil his credit with his tailor. Yes, he shall have my niece with her fortune, he shall.

FOIBLE. He! I hope to see him lodge in Ludgate first, and angle into Blackfriars for brass farthings with an old mitten.

LADY WISHFORT. Ay dear Foible; thank thee for that, dear Foible. He has put me out of all patience. I shall never recompose my features to receive Sir Rowland with any economy of face. This wretch has fretted me that I am absolutely decayed. Look, Foible.

FOIBLE. Your ladyship has frowned a little too rashly, indeed, madam. There are some cracks discernible in the white varnish.

LADY WISHFORT. Let me see the glass. Cracks, say'st thou? Why I am arrantly flayed. I look like an old peeled wall. Thou must repair me Foible, before Sir Rowland comes, or I shall never keep up to my picture.

FOIBLE. I warrant you, madam. A little art once made your picture like you, and now a little of the same art must make you like your picture. Your picture must sit for you, madam.

LADY WISHFORT. But art thou sure Sir Rowland will not fail to come? Or will a' not fail when he does come? Will he be importunate, Foible, and push? For if he should not be importunate, I shall never break decorums. I shall die with confusion, if I am forced to advance – oh no, I can never advance. I shall swoon if he should expect advances. No, I hope Sir Rowland is better bred than to put a lady to the necessity of breaking her forms. I won't be too coy neither – I won't give him despair – but a little disdain is not amiss; a little scorn is alluring.

FOIBLE. A little scorn becomes your ladyship.

LADY WISHFORT. Yes, but tenderness becomes me best – a sort of a dyingness. You see that picture has a sort of a – ha, Foible? A swimminess in the eyes. Yes, I'll look so – my niece affects it, but she wants features. Is Sir Rowland handsome? Let my toilet be removed – I'll dress above. I'll receive Sir Rowland here. Is he handsome? Don't answer me. I won't know; I'll be surprised. I'll be taken by surprise.

FOIBLE. By storm, madam. Sir Rowland's a brisk man.

LADY WISHFORT. Is he! Oh then he'll importune, if he's a brisk man. I shall save decorums if Sir Rowland importunes. I have a mortal terror at the apprehension of offending against decorums. Nothing but importunity can surmount decorums. Oh, I'm glad he's a brisk man. Let my things be removed, good Foible. (*Exit.*)

Enter MRS FAINALL.

MRS FAINALL. Oh Foible, I have been in a fright, lest I should come too late. That devil Marwood saw you in the park with Mirabell, and I'm afraid will discover it to my lady.

FOIBLE. Discover what, madam?

MRS FAINALL. Nay, nay, put not on that strange face. I am privy to the whole design, and know that Waitwell, to whom thou wert this morning married, is to personate Mirabell's uncle, and as such, winning my lady, to involve her in those difficulties from which Mirabell only must release her, by his making his conditions to have my cousin and her fortune left to her own disposal.

FOIBLE. Oh dear madam, I beg your pardon. It was not my confidence in your ladyship that was deficient; but I thought the former good correspondence between your ladyship and Mr Mirabell might have hindered his communicating this secret.

MRS FAINALL. Dear Foible, forget that.

FOIBLE. Oh dear madam, Mr Mirabell is such a sweet winning gentleman – but your ladyship is the pattern of generosity. Sweet lady, to be so good! Mr Mirabell cannot choose but be grateful. I find your ladyship has his heart still. Now, madam, I can safely tell your ladyship our success. Mrs Marwood had told my lady, but I warrant I managed myself. I turned it all for the better. I told my lady that Mr Mirabell railed at her. I laid horrid things to his charge, I'll vow; and my lady is so incensed, that she'll be contracted to Sir Rowland tonight, she says. I warrant I worked her up, that he may have her for asking for, as they say of a Welsh maidenhead.

MRS FAINALL. Oh rare Foible!

FOIBLE. Madam, I beg your ladyship to acquaint Mr Mirabell of his success. I would be seen as little as possible to speak to him. Besides, I believe Madam Marwood watches me. She has a month's mind, but I know Mr Mirabell can't abide her. (*Enter* FOOTMAN.) John, remove my lady's toilet. Madam, your servant. My lady is so impatient, I fear she'll come for me if I stay.

MRS FAINALL. I'll go with you up the back stairs, lest I should meet her.

Exeunt.

Enter MRS MARWOOD.

MRS MARWOOD. Indeed, Mrs Engine, is it thus with you? Are you become a go-between of this importance? Yes, I shall watch you. Why this wench is the *passe-partout*, a very master key to everybody's strongbox. My friend Fainall, have you carried it so swimmingly? I thought there was something in it; but it seems it's over with you. Your loathing is not from a want of appetite then, but from a surfeit. Else you could never be so cool to fall from a principal to be an assistant; to procure for him! 'A pattern of generosity,' that I confess. Well, Mr Fainall, you have met with your match. Oh man, man! Woman, woman! The devil's an ass; if I were a painter, I would draw him like an idiot, a driveller, with a bib and bells. Man should have his head and horns, and woman the rest of him. Poor simple fiend! 'Madam Marwood has a month's mind, but he can't abide her.' 'Twere better for him you had not been his confessor in that affair, without you could have kept his counsel closer. I shall not prove another pattern of generosity and stalk for him, till he takes his stand to aim at a fortune. He has not obliged me to that with those excesses of himself; and now I'll have none of him. Here comes the good lady, panting ripe, with a heart full of hope and a head full of care, like any chemist upon the day of projection.

Enter LADY WISHFORT.

LADY WISHFORT. O dear Marwood, what shall I say for this rude forgetfulness? But my dear friend is all goodness.

MRS MARWOOD. No apologies, dear madam. I have been very well entertained.

LADY WISHFORT. As I'm a person, I am in a very chaos to think I should so forget myself. But I have such an olio of affairs really I know not what to do. (*Calls.*) Foible! I expect my nephew, Sir Wilfull, every moment too – why, Foible – he means to travel for improvement.

MRS MARWOOD. Methinks Sir Wilfull should rather think of marrying than travelling at his years. I hear he is turned of forty.

LADY WISHFORT. Oh, he's in less danger of being spoiled by his travels. I am against my nephew's marrying too young. It will be time enough when he comes back and has acquired discretion to choose for himself.

MRS MARWOOD. Methinks Mrs Millamant and he would make a very fit match. He may travel afterwards. 'Tis a thing very usual with young gentlemen.

LADY WISHFORT. I promise you I have thought on't; and since 'tis your judgment, I'll think on't again, I assure you I will; I value your judgment extremely. On my word, I'll propose it.

Enter FOIBLE.

Come, come Foible, I had forgot my nephew will be here before dinner. I must make haste.

FOIBLE. Mr Witwoud and Mr Petulant are come to dine with your ladyship.

LADY WISHFORT. Oh dear, I can't appear till I'm dressed. Dear Marwood, shall I be free with you again, and beg you to entertain 'em? I'll make all imaginable haste. Dear friend, excuse me.

Exit LADY WISHFORT *and* FOIBLE.

Enter MRS MILLAMANT *and* MINCING.

MILLAMANT. Sure never anything was so unbred as that odious
man. Marwood, your servant.

MRS MARWOOD. You have a colour; what's the matter?

MILLAMANT. That horrid fellow, Petulant, has provoked me into
a flame. I have broke my fan! Mincing, lend me yours; is not all
the powder out of my hair?

MRS MARWOOD. No. What has he done?

MILLAMANT. Nay, he has done nothing; he has only talked.
Nay, he has said nothing neither; but he has contradicted everything that has been said. For my part, I thought Witwoud and
he would have quarrelled.

MINCING. I vow mem, I thought once they would have fit.

MILLAMANT. Well, 'tis a lamentable thing, I'll swear, that one
has not the liberty of choosing one's acquaintance as one does
one's clothes.

MRS MARWOOD. If we had the liberty, we should be as weary
of one set of acquaintance, though never so good, as we are of
one suit, though never so fine. A fool and a doily stuff would
now and then find days of grace, and be worn for variety.

MILLAMANT. I could consent to wear 'em, if they would wear
alike, but fools never wear out – they are such *drap-du-Berry*
things, without one could give 'em to one's chambermaid after
a day or two.

MRS MARWOOD. 'Twere better so indeed. Or what think you
of the playhouse? A fine gay glossy fool should be given there,
like a new masking habit, after the masquerade is over, and
we have done with the disguise. For a fool's visit is always a
disguise, and never admitted by a woman of wit but to blind
her affair with a lover of sense. If you would but appear
barefaced now, and own Mirabell, you might as easily put off
Petulant and Witwoud as your hood and scarf. And indeed 'tis
time, for the town has found it; the secret is grown too big for
the pretence. 'Tis like Mrs Primly's great belly; she may lace it
down before, but it burnishes on her hips. Indeed, Millamant,

you can no more conceal it than my Lady Strammel can her face, that goodly face, which in defiance of her Rhenish-wine tea, will not be comprehended in a mask.

MILLAMANT. I'll take my death, Marwood, you are more censorious than a decayed beauty, or a discarded toast; Mincing, tell the men they may come up. My aunt is not dressing; their folly is less provoking than your malice. (*Exit* MINCING.) 'The town has found it.' What has it found? That Mirabell loves me is no more a secret than it is a secret that you discovered it to my aunt, or than the reason why you discovered it is a secret.

MRS MARWOOD. You are nettled.

MILLAMANT. You're mistaken. Ridiculous!

MRS MARWOOD. Indeed my dear, you'll tear another fan if you don't mitigate those violent airs.

MILLAMANT. Oh silly! Ha, ha, ha! I could laugh immoderately. Poor Mirabell! His constancy to me has quite destroyed his complaisance for all the world beside. I swear, I never enjoined it him to be so coy. If I had the vanity to think he would obey me, I would command him to show more gallantry. 'Tis hardly well bred to be so particular on one hand, and so insensible on the other. But I despair to prevail, and so let him follow his own way. Ha, ha, ha! Pardon me, dear creature, I must laugh, ha, ha, ha, though I grant you 'tis a little barbarous, ha, ha, ha!

MRS MARWOOD. What pity 'tis, so much fine raillery, and delivered with so significant gesture, should be so unhappily directed to miscarry.

MILLAMANT. Ha? Dear creature, I ask your pardon – I swear I did not mind you.

MRS MARWOOD. Mr Mirabell and you both may think it a thing impossible, when I shall tell him, by telling you –

MILLAMANT. Oh dear, what? For it is the same thing if I hear it, ha, ha, ha!

MRS MARWOOD. That I detest him, hate him, madam.

MILLAMANT. Oh madam, why so do I – and yet the creature loves me, ha, ha, ha! How can one forbear laughing to think of it? I am a sybil if I am not amazed to think what he can see in me. I'll take my death, I think you are handsomer – and within a year or two as young. If you could but stay for me, I should overtake you – but that cannot be. Well, that thought makes me melancholy. Now I'll be sad.

MRS MARWOOD. Your merry note may be changed sooner than you think.

MILLAMANT. D'ye say so? Then I'm resolved I'll have a song to keep up my spirits.

Enter MINCING.

MINCING. The gentlemen stay but to comb, madam, and will wait on you.

MILLAMANT. Desire Mrs – , that is in the next room, to sing the song I would have learned yesterday. You shall hear it madam not that there's any great matter in it, but 'tis agreeable to my humour.

Song, set by Mr John Eccles, and sung by Mrs Hodgson.

I

Love's but the frailty of the mind,
    When 'tis not with ambition joined;
A sickly flame, which if not fed, expires;
And feeding, wastes in self-consuming fires.

II

'Tis not to wound a wanton boy
    Or am'rous youth, that gives the joy;
But 'tis the glory to have pierced a swain,
For whom inferior beauties sighed in vain.

III

Then I alone the conquest prize,
    When I insult a rival's eyes;
If there's delight in love, 'tis when I see
That heart which others bleed for, bleed for me.

Enter PETULANT *and* WITWOUD.

MILLAMANT. Is your animosity composed, gentlemen?

WITWOUD. Raillery, raillery, madam; we have no animosity. We hit off a little wit now and then, but no animosity. The falling out of wits is like the falling out of lovers; we agree in the main, like treble and bass. Ha, Petulant?

PETULANT. Ay, in the main – but when I have a humour to contradict.

WITWOUD. Ay, when he has a humour to contradict, then I contradict too. What, I know my cue. Then we contradict one another like two battledores; for contradictions beget one another like Jews.

PETULANT. If he says black's black, if I have a humour to say 'tis blue, let that pass; all's one for that. If I have a humour to prove it, it must be granted.

WITWOUD. Not positively must but it may, it may.

PETULANT. Yes, it positively must, upon proof positive.

WITWOUD. Ay, upon proof positive it must; but upon proof presumptive it only may. That's a logical distinction now, madam.

MRS MARWOOD. I perceive your debates are of importance and very learnedly handled.

PETULANT. Importance is one thing, and learning's another; but a debate's a debate, that I assert.

WITWOUD. Petulant's an enemy to learning; he relies altogether on his parts.

PETULANT. No, I'm no enemy to learning; it hurts not me.

MRS MARWOOD. That's a sign indeed it's no enemy to you.

PETULANT. No, no, it's no enemy to anybody but them that have it.

MILLAMANT. Well, an illiterate man's my aversion. I wonder at the impudence of any illiterate man to offer to make love.

WITWOUD. That I confess I wonder at too.

MILLAMANT. Ah! to marry an ignorant that can hardly read or write.

PETULANT. Why should a man be ever the further from being married though he can't read, any more than he is from being hanged? The Ordinary's paid for setting the psalm, and the parish priest for reading the ceremony. And for the rest which is to follow in both cases, a man may do it without book so all's one for that.

MILLAMANT. D'ye hear the creature? Lord, here's company; I'll be gone.

Exeunt MILLAMANT *and* MINCING.

WITWOUD. In the name of Bartlemew and his fair, what have we here?

MRS MARWOOD. 'Tis your brother, I fancy. Don't you know him?

WITWOUD. Not I – yes, I think it is he – I've almost forgot him; I have not seen him since the Revolution.

Enter SIR WILFULL WITWOUD *in a country riding habit, and* SERVANT *to* LADY WISHFORT.

SERVANT. Sir, my lady's dressing. Here's company, if you please to walk in, in the mean time.

SIR WILFULL. Dressing! What, it's but morning here, I warrant with you, in London. We should count it towards afternoon in our parts, down in Shropshire. Why then, belike my aunt han't dined yet – ha, friend?

SERVANT. Your aunt, sir?

SIR WILFULL. My aunt, sir, yes my aunt, sir, and your lady, sir; your lady is my aunt, sir. Why, what, dost thou not know me, friend? Why then send somebody here that does. How long hast thou lived with thy lady, fellow, ha?

SERVANT. A week, sir; longer than anybody in the house, except my lady's woman.

SIR WILFULL. Why then, belike thou dost not know thy lady if thou seest her, ha, friend?

SERVANT. Why truly, sir, I cannot safely swear to her face in a morning, before she is dressed. 'Tis like I may give a shrewd guess at her by this time.

SIR WILFULL. Well, prithee try what thou canst do; if thou canst not guess, enquire her out, dost hear fellow? And tell her, her nephew, Sir Wilfull Witwoud, is in the house.

SERVANT. I shall, sir.

SIR WILFULL. Hold ye, hear me, friend; a word with you in your ear. Prithee who are these gallants?

SERVANT. Really sir, I can't tell; here come so many here, 'tis hard to know 'em all.

Exit SERVANT.

SIR WILFULL. Oons, this fellow knows less than a starling; I don't think a' knows his own name.

MRS MARWOOD. Mr Witwoud, your brother is not behindhand in forgetfulness; I fancy he has forgot you too.

WITWOUD. I hope so. The devil take him that remembers first, I say.

SIR WILFULL. Save you, gentlemen and lady.

MRS MARWOOD. For shame, Mr Witwoud; why won't you speak to him? And you, sir.

WITWOUD. Petulant, speak.

PETULANT. And you, sir.

SIR WILFULL. No offence, I hope. (*Salutes* MRS MARWOOD.)

MRS MARWOOD. No, sure sir.

WITWOUD. This is a vile dog, I see that already. No offence! Ha, ha, ha! To him, to him, Petulant! Smoke him.

PETULANT. It seems as if you had come a journey, sir, hem, hem. (*Surveying him round.*)

SIR WILFULL. Very likely, sir, that it may seem so.

PETULANT. No offence, I hope, sir.

WITWOUD. Smoke the boots, the boots, Petulant, the boots! Ha, ha, ha.

SIR WILFULL. Maybe not, sir; thereafter as 'tis meant, sir.

PETULANT. Sir, I presume upon the information of your boots.

SIR WILFULL. Why, 'tis like you may, sir. If you are not satisfied with the information of my boots, sir, if you will step to the stable, you may enquire further of my horse, sir!

PETULANT. Your horse, sir! Your horse is an ass, sir!

SIR WILFULL. Do you speak by way of offence, sir?

MRS MARWOOD. The gentleman's merry, that's all, sir. (*Aside.*) 'Slife, we shall have a quarrel betwixt an horse and an ass, before they find one another out. (*Aloud.*) You must not take anything amiss from your friends, sir. You are among your friends here, though it may be you don't know it. If I am not mistaken, you are Sir Wilfull Witwoud.

SIR WILFULL. Right, lady; I am Sir Wilfull Witwoud, so I write myself; no offence to anybody, I hope; and nephew to the Lady Wishfort of this mansion.

MRS MARWOOD. Don t you know this gentleman, sir?

SIR WILFULL. Hum! What, sure 'tis not – yea, by'r lady, but 'tis. 'S'heart, I know not whether 'tis or no – yea but 'tis by the Rekin. Brother Anthony! What Tony, i'faith! What, dost thou not know me? By'r Lady, nor I thee, thou art so becravatted, and beperiwigged. 'S'heart, why dost not speak? Art thou o'erjoyed?

WITWOUD. Odso, brother, is it you? Your servant, brother.

SIR WILFULL. Your servant! Why, yours, sir. Your servant again, 's'heart, and your friend and servant to that, and a (*Puff*.) and a flapdragon for your service, sir; and a hare's foot, and a hare's scut for your service, sir, an you be so cold and so courtly!

WITWOUD. No offence, I hope, brother.

SIR WILFULL. 'S'heart, sir, but there is, and much offence. A pox, is this your Inns o' Court breeding, not to know your friends and your relations, your elders, and your betters?

WITWOUD. Why, brother Wilfull of Salop, you may be as short as a Shrewsbury cake, if you please, but I tell you, 'tis not modish to know relations in town. You think you're in the country, where great lubberly brothers slobber and kiss one another when they meet, like a call of serjeants. 'Tis not the fashion here; 'tis not indeed, dear brother.

SIR WILFULL. The fashion's a fool; and you're a fop, dear brother. 'S'heart, I've suspected this. By'r Lady I conjectured you were a fop since you began to change the style of your letters, and write in a scrap of paper gilt round the edges, no broader than a subpoena. I might expect this, when you left off 'Honoured Brother', and 'hoping you are in good health', and so forth, to begin with a 'Rat me, knight, I'm so sick of a last night's debauch'; ods heart, and then tell a familiar tale of a cock and a bull, and a whore and a bottle, and so conclude. You could write news before you were out of your time, when you lived with honest Pumplenose the attorney of Furnival's Inn; you could entreat to be remembered then to your friends round the Rekin. We could have gazettes then, and *Dawk's Letter*, and the weekly bill, till of late days.

PETULANT. 'Slife, Witwoud, were you ever an attorney's clerk? Of the family of the Furnivals? Ha, ha, ha!

WITWOUD. Ay, ay, but that was for a while. Not long, not long; pshaw, I was not in my own power then. An orphan, and this fellow was my guardian; ay, ay, I was glad to consent to that man to come to London. He had the disposal of me then. If I had not agreed to that, I might have been bound 'prentice to a felt-maker in Shrewsbury; this fellow would have bound me to a maker of felts!

SIR WILFULL. 'S'heart, and better than to be bound to a maker of fops, where, I suppose, you have served your time, and now you may set up for yourself.

MRS MARWOOD. You intend to travel, sir, as I'm informed.

SIR WILFULL. Belike I may, madam. I may chance to sail upon the salt seas, if my mind hold.

PETULANT. And the wind serve.

SIR WILFULL. Serve or not serve, I shan't ask licence of you, sir; nor the weathercock your companion. I direct my discourse to the lady, sir. 'Tis like my aunt may have told you, madam. Yes, I have settled my concerns, I may say now, and am minded to see foreign parts. If and how that the peace holds, whereby, that is, taxes abate.

MRS MARWOOD. I thought you had designed for France at all adventures.

SIR WILFULL. I can't tell that; 'tis like I may, and 'tis like I may not. I am somewhat dainty in making a resolution, because when I make it I keep it. I don't stand shill I, shall I, then; if I say't, I'll do't. But I have thoughts to tarry a small matter in town, to learn somewhat of your lingo first, before I cross the seas. I'd gladly have a spice of your French, as they say, whereby to hold discourse in foreign countries.

MRS MARWOOD. Here is an academy in town for that use.

SIR WILFULL. There is? 'Tis like there may.

MRS MARWOOD. No doubt you will return very much improved.

WITWOUD. Yes, refined, like a Dutch skipper from a whale-fishing.

Enter LADY WISHFORT *and* FAINALL.

LADY WISHFORT. Nephew, you are welcome.

SIR WILFULL. Aunt, your servant.

FAINALL. Sir Wilfull, your most faithful servant.

SIR WILFULL. Cousin Fainall, give me your hand.

LADY WISHFORT. Cousin Witwoud, your servant; Mr Petulant, your servant. Nephew, you are welcome again. Will you drink anything after your journey, nephew, before you eat? Dinner's almost ready.

SIR WILFULL. I'm very well, I thank you, aunt; however, I thank you for your courteous offer. 'S'heart, I was afraid you would have been in the fashion too, and have remembered to have forgot your relations. Here's your cousin Tony, belike I mayn't call him brother for fear of offence.

LADY WISHFORT. Oh he's a rallier, nephew – my cousin's a wit, and your great wits always rally their best friends to choose. When you have been abroad, nephew, you'll understand raillery better.

FAINALL *and* MRS MARWOOD *talk apart.*

SIR WILFULL. Why then let him hold his tongue in the meantime, and rail when that day comes.

Enter MINCING.

MINCING. Mem, I come to acquaint your la'ship that dinner is impatient.

SIR WILFULL. Impatient? Why then belike it won't stay till I pull off my boots. Sweetheart, can you help me to a pair of slippers? My man's with his horses, I warrant.

LADY WISHFORT. Fie, fie, nephew, you would not pull off your boots here. Go down into the hall; dinner shall stay for you. My nephew's a little unbred; you'll pardon him, madam. Gentlemen, will you walk? Marwood?

MRS MARWOOD. I'll follow you, madam, before Sir Wilfull is ready.

MRS MARWOOD *and* FAINALL *remain.*

FAINALL. Why then, Foible's a bawd, an errant, rank, match-making bawd. And I, it seems, am a husband, a rank husband; and my wife a very arrant, rank wife – all in the way of the world. 'Sdeath, to be an anticipated cuckold, a cuckold in embryo! Sure I was born with budding antlers like a young satyr, or a citizen's child. 'Sdeath to be outwitted, to be out-jilted, out-matrimonied! If I had kept my speed like a stag, 'twere somewhat, but to crawl after, with my horns, like a snail, and outstripped by my wife – 'tis scurvy wedlock.

MRS MARWOOD. Then shake it off. You have often wished for an opportunity to part, and now you have it. But first, prevent their plot; the half of Millamant's fortune is too considerable to be parted with, to a foe, to Mirabell.

FAINALL. Damn him! That had been mine, had you not made that fond discovery. That had been forfeited, had they been married. My wife had added lustre to my horns by that increase of fortune; I could have worn 'em tipped with gold, though my forehead had been furnished like a deputy lieutenant's hall.

MRS MARWOOD. They may prove a cap of maintenance to you still, if you can away with your wife. And she's no worse than when you had her – I dare swear she had given up her game before she was married.

FAINALL. Hum! That may be; she might throw up her cards; but I'll be hanged if she did not put Pam in her pocket.

MRS MARWOOD. You married her to keep you; and if you can contrive to have her keep you better than you expected, why should you not keep her longer than you intended?

FAINALL. The means, the means.

MRS MARWOOD. Discover to my lady your wife's conduct; threaten to part with her. My lady loves her, and will come to any composition to save her reputation. Take the opportunity of breaking it, just upon the discovery of this imposture. My lady will be enraged beyond bounds, and sacrifice niece and fortune and all at that conjuncture. And let me alone to keep her warm; if she should flag in her part, I will not fail to prompt her.

FAINALL. Faith, this has an appearance.

MRS MARWOOD. I'm sorry I hinted to my lady to endeavour a match between Millamant and Sir Wilfull; that may be an obstacle.

FAINALL. Oh, for that matter leave me to manage him; I'll disable him for that. He will drink like a Dane; after dinner, I'll set his hand in.

MRS MARWOOD. Well, how do you stand affected towards your lady?

FAINALL. Why, faith, I'm thinking of it. Let me see. I am married already, so that's over. My wife has played the jade with me; well, that's over too. I never loved her, or if I had, why that would have been over too by this time. Jealous of her I cannot be, for I am certain; so there's an end of jealousy. Weary of her I am, and shall be. No, there's no end of that; no, no, that were too much to hope. Thus far concerning my repose. Now for my reputation. As to my own, I married not for it; so that's out of the question. And as to my part in my wife's, why she had parted with hers before; so bringing none to me, she can take none from me. 'Tis against all rule of play that I should lose to one who has not wherewithal to stake.

MRS MARWOOD. Besides, you forget, marriage is honourable.

FAINALL. Hum! Faith, and that's well thought on; marriage is honourable, as you say; and if so, wherefore should cuckoldom be a discredit, being derived from so honourable a root?

MRS MARWOOD. Nay I know not; if the root be honourable, why not the branches?

FAINALL. So, so; why this point's clear. Well, how do we proceed?

MRS MARWOOD. I will contrive a letter which shall be delivered to my lady at the time when that rascal who is to act Sir Rowland is with her. It shall come as from an unknown hand – for the less I appear to know of the truth, the better I can play the incendiary. Besides, I would not have Foible provoked if I could

help it, because you know she knows some passages. Nay, I
expect all will come out; but let the mine be sprung first, and
then I care not if I'm discovered.

FAINALL. If the worst come to the worst, I'll turn my wife to
grass. I have already a deed of settlement of the best part of her
estate, which I wheedled out of her; and that you shall partake
at least.

MRS MARWOOD. I hope you are convinced that I hate Mirabell
now; you'll be no more jealous?

FAINALL. Jealous, no – by this kiss. Let husbands be jealous; but
let the lover still believe. Or, if he doubt, let it be only to
endear his pleasure and prepare the joy that follows, when he
proves his mistress true. But let husbands' doubts convert to
endless jealousy; or if they have belief let it corrupt to
superstition and blind credulity. I am single, and will herd no
more with 'em. True, I wear the badge; but I'll disown the
order. And since I take my leave of 'em, I care not if I leave
'em a common motto to their common crest:

All husbands must or pain or shame endure;
The wise too jealous are, fools too secure.

Exeunt.

ACT FOUR

Scene One

Scene continues.

Enter LADY WISHFORT *and* FOIBLE.

LADY WISHFORT. Is Sir Rowland coming, sayest thou, Foible? and are things in order?

FOIBLE. Yes madam. I have put waxlights in the sconces, and placed the footmen in a row in the hall, in their best liveries, with the coachman and postilion to fill up the equipage.

LADY WISHFORT. Have you pullvilled the coachman and postilion, that they may not stink of the stable when Sir Rowland comes by?

FOIBLE. Yes, madam.

LADY WISHFORT. And are the dancers and the music ready, that he may be entertained in all points with correspondence to his passion?

FOIBLE. All is ready, madam.

LADY WISHFORT. And – well – and how do I look, Foible?

FOIBLE. Most killing well, madam.

LADY WISHFORT. Well, and how shall I receive him? In what figure shall I give his heart the first impression? There is a great deal in the first impression. Shall I sit? No, I won't sit – I'll walk; ay, I'll walk from the door upon his entrance, and then turn full upon him. No, that will be too sudden. I'll lie – ay, I'll lie down. I'll receive him in my little dressing-room; there's a couch – yes, yes, I'll give the first impression on a couch. I won't lie neither, but loll and lean upon one elbow, with one foot a little dangling off, jogging in a thoughtful way. Yes – and then as soon as he appears, start, ay, start and be surprised, and rise to meet him in a pretty disorder. Yes. Oh, nothing is more alluring than a levée from a couch in some confusion. It shows the foot to advantage, and furnishes with blushes and recomposing airs beyond comparison. Hark! There's a coach.

FOIBLE. 'Tis he, madam.

LADY WISHFORT. Oh dear, has my nephew made his addresses to Millamant? I ordered him.

FOIBLE. Sir Wilfull is set in to drinking, madam, in the parlour.

LADY WISHFORT. Ods my life, I'll send him to her. Call her down, Foible; bring her hither. I'll send him as I go. When they are together, then come to me, Foible, that I may not be too long alone with Sir Rowland.

Exit.

Enter MRS MILLAMANT, *and* MRS FAINALL.

FOIBLE. Madam, I stayed here to tell your ladyship that Mr Mirabell has waited this half hour for an opportunity to talk with you, though my lady's orders were to leave you and Sir Wilfull together. Shall I tell Mr Mirabell that you are at leisure?

MILLAMANT. No – what would the dear man have? I am thoughtful, and would amuse myself – bid him come another time.

There never yet was woman made,
Nor shall, but to be curs'd.

(*Repeating and walking about.*) That's hard!

MRS FAINALL. You are very fond of Sir John Suckling today, Millamant, and the poets.

MILLAMANT. He? Ay, and filthy verses; so I am.

FOIBLE. Sir Wilfull is coming, madam. Shall I send Mr Mirabell away?

MILLAMANT. Ay, if you please, Foible, send him away – or send him hither just as you will, dear Foible. I think I'll see him; shall I? Ay, let the wretch come. (*Exit* FOIBLE.)

Thyrsis a youth of the inspir'd train –

Repeating.

Dear Fainall, entertain Sir Wilfull. Thou hast philosophy to undergo a fool, thou art married and hast patience. I would confer with my own thoughts.

MRS FAINALL. I am obliged to you, that you would make me your proxy in this affair; but I have business of my own.

Enter SIR WILFULL.

O Sir Wilfull, you are come at the critical instant. There's your mistress up to the ears in love and contemplation; pursue your point, now or never.

SIR WILFULL. Yes; my aunt would have it so. I would gladly have been encouraged with a bottle or two, because I'm somewhat wary at first, before I am acquainted. But I hope after a time, I shall break my mind – that is, upon further acquaintance – so for the present, cousin, I'll take my leave. If so be you'll be so kind to make my excuse, I'll return to my company

This while MILLAMANT *walks about repeating to herself.*

MRS FAINALL. Oh fie, Sir Wilfull! What, you must not be daunted.

SIR WILFULL. Daunted? No, that's not it, it is not so much for that for if so be that I set on't, I'll do't. But only for the present, 'tis sufficient till further acquaintance, that's all – your servant.

MRS FAINALL. Nay, I'll swear you shall never lose so favourable an opportunity, if I can help it. I'll leave you together and lock the door.

Exit.

SIR WILFULL. Nay, nay cousin – I have forgot my gloves – what d'ye do? 'S'heart, a' has locked the door indeed, I think! Nay, cousin Fainall, open the door! Pshaw, what a vixen trick is this? Nay, now a' has seen me too. Cousin, I made bold to pass through as it were – I think this door's enchanted.

MILLAMANT (*repeating*).
  I prithee spare me, gentle boy,
  Press me no more for that slight toy.

SIR WILFULL. Anan? Cousin, your servant.

MILLAMANT. That foolish trifle of a heart –

  Sir Wilfull!

SIR WILFULL. Yes – your servant. No offence I hope, cousin.

MILLAMANT (*repeating*).
  I swear it will not do its part,
  Tho' thou dost thine, employ'st thy power and art.

  Natural, easy Suckling!

SIR WILFULL. Anan? Suckling? No such suckling neither, cousin, nor stripling; I thank heaven, I'm no minor.

MILLAMANT. Ah rustic! Ruder than Gothic.

SIR WILFULL. Well, well, I shall understand your lingo one of these days, cousin; in the meanwhile, I must answer in plain English.

MILLAMANT. Have you any business with me, Sir Wilfull?

SIR WILFULL. Not at present, cousin. Yes, I made bold to see, to come and know if that how you were disposed to fetch a walk this evening, if so be that I might not be troublesome, I would have sought a walk with you.

MILLAMANT. A walk? What then?

SIR WILFULL. Nay, nothing – only for the walk's sake, that's all.

MILLAMANT. I nauseate walking; 'tis a country diversion, I loathe the country and everything that relates to it.

SIR WILFULL. Indeed! Hah! Look ye, look ye, you do? Nay, 'tis like you may. Here are choice of pastimes here in town, as plays and the like; that must be confessed indeed.

MILLAMANT. Ah, *l'étourdie!* I hate the town too.

SIR WILFULL. Dear heart, that's much. Hah! that you should hate 'em both! Hah! 'Tis like you may; there are some can't relish the town, and others can't away with the country. 'Tis like you may be one of those, cousin.

MILLAMANT. Ha, ha, ha! Yes, 'tis like I may. You have nothing further to say to me?

SIR WILFULL. Not at present, cousin. 'Tis like when I have an opportunity to be more private, I may break my mind in some measure – I conjecture you partly guess – however, that's as time shall try; but spare to speak and spare to speed, as they say.

MILLAMANT. If it is of no great importance, Sir Wilfull, you will oblige me to leave me; I have just now a little business

SIR WILFULL. Enough, enough, cousin; yes, yes, all a case when you're disposed, when you're disposed. Now's as well as another time; and another time as well as now. All's one for that. Yes, yes, if your concerns call you, there's no haste; it will keep cold, as they say. Cousin, your servant. I think this door's locked.

MILLAMANT. You may go this way, sir.

SIR WILFULL. Your servant; then with your leave I'll return to my company. (*Exit.*)

MILLAMANT. Ay, ay; ha, ha, ha!

Like Phoebus sung the no less am'rous boy .

Enter MIRABELL.

MIRABELL.

– Like Daphne she as lovely and as coy.

Do you lock yourself up from me, to make my search more curious? Or is this pretty artifice contrived, to signify that here the chase must end and my pursuit be crowned, for you can fly no further?

MILLAMANT. Vanity! No – I'll fly and be followed to the last
moment. Though I am upon the very verge of matrimony,
I expect you should solicit me as much as if I were wavering
at the grate of a monastery, with one foot over the threshold.
I'll be solicited to the very last, nay, and afterwards.

MIRABELL. What, after the last?

MILLAMANT. Oh, I should think I was poor and had nothing to
bestow if I were reduced to an inglorious ease, and freed from
the agreeable fatigues of solicitation.

MIRABELL. But do not you know that when favours are con-
ferred upon instant and tedious solicitation, that they diminish
in their value, and that both the giver loses the grace, and the
receiver lessens his pleasure?

MILLAMANT. It may be in things of common application, but
never sure in love. Oh, I hate a lover that can dare to think
he draws a moment's air independent on the bounty of his mistress. There is not so impudent a thing in nature as the saucy
look of an assured man, confident of success. The pedantic
arrogance of a very husband has not so pragmatical an air.
Ah! I'll never marry, unless I am first made sure of my will
and pleasure.

MIRABELL. Would you have 'em both before marriage? Or will
you be contented with the first now, and stay for the other till
after grace?

MILLAMANT. Ah, don't be impertinent. My dear liberty, shall
I leave thee? My faithful solitude, my darling contemplation,
must I bid you then adieu? Ay-h adieu, my morning thoughts,
agreeable wakings, indolent slumbers, all ye *douceurs*, ye *sommeils
du matin*, adieu. I can't do't, 'tis more than impossible. Positively
Mirabell, I'll lie abed in a morning as long as I please.

MIRABELL. Then I'll get up in a morning as early as I please.

MILLAMANT. Ah, idle creature, get up when you will – and d'ye
hear, I won't be called names after I'm married; positively I
won't be called names.

MIRABELL. Names!

MILLAMANT. Ay, as wife, spouse, my dear, joy, jewel, love, sweetheart, and the rest of that nauseous cant in which men and their wives are so fulsomely familiar. I shall never bear that. Good Mirabell, don't let us be familiar or fond, nor kiss before folks, like my Lady Fadler and Sir Francis; nor go to Hyde Park together the first Sunday in a new chariot, to provoke eyes and whispers, and then never to be seen there together again, as if we were proud of one another the first week, and ashamed of one another for ever after. Let us never visit together, nor go to a play together, but let us be very strange and well-bred; let us be as strange as if we had been married a great while, and as well bred as if we were not married at all.

MIRABELL. Have you any more conditions to offer? Hitherto your demands are pretty reasonable.

MILLAMANT. Trifles. As liberty to pay and receive visits to and from whom I please, to write and receive letters, without interrogatories or wry faces on your part. To wear what I please, and choose conversation with regard only to my own taste; to have no obligation upon me to converse with wits that I don't like, because they are your acquaintance, or to be intimate with fools, because they may be your relations. Come to dinner when I please; dine in my dressing-room when I'm out of humour, without giving a reason. To have my closet inviolate; to be sole empress of my tea-table, which you must never presume to approach without first asking leave. And lastly, wherever I am, you shall always knock at the door before you come in. These articles subscribed, if I continue to endure you a little longer, I may by degrees dwindle into a wife.

MIRABELL. Your bill of fare is something advanced in this latter account. Well, have I liberty to offer conditions – that when you are dwindled into a wife, I may not be beyond measure enlarged into a husband?

MILLAMANT. You have free leave; propose your utmost, speak and spare not.

MIRABELL. I thank you. *Inprimis* then, I covenant that your
acquaintance be general; that you admit no sworn confidante,
or intimate of your own sex; no she-friend to screen her affairs
under your countenance and tempt you to make trial of a mutual
secrecy. No decoy duck to wheedle you a fop, scrambling to
the play in a mask; then bring you home in a pretended fright,
when you think you shall be found out – and rail at me for
missing the play, and disappointing the frolic, which you had
to pick me up and prove my constancy.

MILLAMANT. Detestable *inprimis!* I go to the play in a mask!

MIRABELL. *Item*, I article that you continue to like your own
face, as long as I shall. And while it passes current with me,
that you endeavour not to new coin it. To which end, together
with all vizards for the day, I prohibit all masks for the night,
made of oiled skins and I know not what – hog's bones, hare's
gall, pig-water, and the marrow of a roasted cat. In short, I
forbid all commerce with the gentlewoman in what-d'ye-call-it
Court. *Item*, I shut my doors against all bawds with baskets, and
pennyworths of muslin, china, fans, atlases, etc. etc. *Item*, when
you shall be breeding –

MILLAMANT. Ah! Name it not.

MIRABELL. Which may be presumed, with a blessing on our
endeavours –

MILLAMANT. Odious endeavours!

MIRABELL. I denounce against all straitlacing, squeezing for a
shape, till you mould my boy's head like a sugarloaf; and
instead of a manchild, make me the father to a crooked billet.
Lastly, to the dominion of the tea-table I submit – but with
proviso that you exceed not in your province, but restrain
yourself to native and simple tea-table drinks, as tea, chocolate
and coffee. As likewise to genuine and authorised tea-table talk,
such as mending of fashions, spoiling reputations, railing at
absent friends, and so forth; but that on no account you
encroach upon the men's prerogative, and presume to drink
healths, or toast fellows; for prevention of which, I banish all

forcign forces, all auxiliaries to the tea-table, as orange-brandy, all aniseed, cinnamon, citron and Barbadoes waters, together with ratafia and the most noble spirit of clary. But for cowslip wine, poppy-water and all dormitives, those I allow. These provisos admitted, in other things I may prove a tractable and complying husband.

MILLAMANT. Oh horrid provisos! Filthy strong waters! I toast fellows, odious men! I hate your odious provisos.

MIRABELL. Then we're agreed. Shall I kiss your hand upon the contract? And here comes one to be a witness to the sealing of the deed.

Enter MRS FAINALL.

MILLAMANT. Fainall, what shall I do? Shall I have him? I think I must have him.

MRS FAINALL. Ay, ay, take him, take him, what should you do?

MILLAMANT. Well then – I'll take my death I'm in a horrid fright – Fainall, I shall never say it – well – I think – I'll endure you.

MRS FAINALL. Fie, fie, have him, have him, and tell him so in plain terms; for I am sure you have a mind to him.

MILLAMANT. Are you? I think I have – and the horrid man looks as if he thought so too. Well, you ridiculous thing you, I'll have you. I won't be kissed, nor I won't be thanked. Here, kiss my hand though. So, hold your tongue now, and don't say a word.

MRS FAINALL. Mirabell, there's a necessity for your obedience; you have neither time to talk nor stay. My mother is coming; and in my conscience if she should see you, would fall into fits, and maybe not recover time enough to return to Sir Rowland, who as Foible tells me is in a fair way to succeed. Therefore spare your ecstasies for another occasion, and slip down the backstairs, where Foible waits to consult you.

MILLAMANT. Ay, go, go. In the meantime I suppose you have said something to please me.

MIRABELL. I am all obedience. (*Exit* MIRABELL.)

MRS FAINALL. Yonder Sir Wilfull's drunk, and so noisy that my
   mother has been forced to leave Sir Rowland to appease him;
   but he answers her only with singing and drinking. What they
   have done by this time I know not, but Petulant and he were
   upon quarrelling as I came by.

MILLAMANT. Well, if Mirabell should not make a good husband,
   I am a lost thing, for I find I love him violently.

MRS FAINALL. So it seems, when you mind not what's said to
   you. If you doubt him, you had best take up with Sir Wilfull.

MILLAMANT. How can you name that superannuated lubber?
   Foh! (*Enter* WITWOUD *from drinking.*)

MRS FAINALL. So, is the fray made up, that you have left em?

WITWOUD. Left 'em? I could stay no longer. I have laughed
   like ten christenings – I am tipsy with laughing. If I had stayed
   any longer I should have burst – I must have been let out and
   pieced in the sides like an unsized camlet. Yes, yes, the fray is
   composed; my lady came in like a *noli prosequi* and stopped their
   proceedings.

MILLAMANT. What was the dispute?

WITWOUD. That's the jest, there was no dispute, they could
   neither of 'em speak for rage, and so fell a-sputtering at one
   another like two roasting apples.

Enter PETULANT *drunk.*

   Now Petulant, all's over, all's well? Gad, my head begins to
   whim it about – why dost thou not speak? Thou art both as
   drunk and as mute as a fish.

PETULANT. Look you, Mrs Millamant, if you can love me, dear
   nymph say it – and that's the conclusion – pass on, or pass off
   that's all.

WITWOUD. Thou hast uttered volumes, folios, in less than
   decimo sexto, my dear Lacedemonian. Sirrah Petulant, thou art
   an epitomiser of words.

PETULANT. Witwoud – you are an annihilator of sense.

WITWOUD. Thou art a retailer of phrases, and dost deal in remnants of remnants, like a maker of pin-cushions – thou art in truth, metaphorically speaking, a speaker of shorthand.

PETULANT. Thou art, without a figure, just one half of an ass, and Baldwin yonder, thy half-brother, is the rest. A gemini of asses split would make just four of you.

WITWOUD. Thou dost bite, my dear mustardseed; kiss me for that.

PETULANT. Stand off! I'll kiss no more males – I have kissed your twin yonder in a humour of reconciliation, till he (*Hiccup.*) rises upon my stomach like a radish.

MILLAMANT. Eh, filthy creature – what was the quarrel?

PETULANT. There was no quarrel – there might have been a quarrel.

WITWOUD. If there had been words enow between 'em to have expressed provocation, they had gone together by the ears like a pair of castanets.

PETULANT. You were the quarrel.

MILLAMANT. Me!

PETULANT. If I have a humour to quarrel, I can make less matters conclude premises. If you are not handsome, what then, if I have a humour to prove it? If I shall have my reward, say so; if not, fight for your face the next time yourself – I'll go sleep.

WITWOUD. Do, wrap thyself up like a woodlouse and dream revenge. And hear me, if thou canst learn to write by tomorrow morning, pen me a challenge. I'll carry it for thee.

PETULANT. Carry your mistress's monkey a spider – go flea dogs, and read romances – I'll go to bed to my maid. (*Exit.*)

MRS FAINALL. He's horridly drunk. How came you all in this pickle?

WITWOUD. A plot, a plot, to get rid of the knight – your husband's advice; but he sneaked off.

Enter LADY WISHFORT *and* SIR WILFULL *drunk.*

LADY WISHFORT. Out upon't, out upon't, at years of discretion, and comport yourself at this rantipole rate.

SIR WILFULL. No offence, aunt.

LADY WISHFORT. Offence? As I'm a person, I'm ashamed of you. Fogh! how you stink of wine! D'ye think my niece will ever endure such a borachio! You're an absolute borachio.

SIR WILFULL. Borachio!

LADY WISHFORT. At a time when you should commence an amour and put your best foot foremost –

SIR WILFULL. 'S'heart, an you grutch me your liquor, make a bill. Give me more drink, and take my purse. (*Sings.*)

> Prithee fill me the glass
> Till it laugh in my face,
> With ale that is potent and mellow;
> He that whines for a lass
> Is an ignorant ass,
> For a bumper has not its fellow.

But if you would have me marry my cousin – say the word, and I'll do't – Wilfull will do't, that's the word – Wilfull will do't; that's my crest – my motto I have forgot.

LADY WISHFORT. My nephew's a little overtaken, cousin, but 'tis with drinking your health. O' my word you are obliged to him.

SIR WILFULL. *In vino veritas* aunt. If I drunk your health today cousin – I am a borachio. But if you have a mind to be married, say the word, and send for the piper, Wilfull will do't. If not, dust it away, and let's have t'other round – Tony! Odsheart, where's Tony? Tony's an honest fellow, but he spits after a bumper, and that's a fault.

Sings.

> We'll drink, and we'll never ha' done, boys,
> Put the glass then around with the sun, boys,
> Let Apollo's example invite us;
> For he's drunk every night,
> And that makes him so bright,
> That he's able next morning to light us.

The sun's a good pimple, an honest soaker, he has a cellar at your Antipodes. If I travel, aunt, I touch at your Antipodes – your Antipodes are a good rascally sort of topsy-turvy fellows – if I had a bumper, I'd stand upon my head and drink a health to 'em. A match or no match, cousin with the hard name? Aunt, Wilfull will do't; if she has her maidenhead, let her look to't – if she has not, let her keep her own counsel in the meantime, and cry out at the nine months' end.

MILLAMANT. Your pardon, madam, I can stay no longer. Sir Wilfull grows very powerful. Egh, how he smells! I shall be overcome if I stay. Come, cousin.

Exeunt MILLAMANT *and* MRS FAINALL.

LADY WISHFORT. Smells! He would poison a tallow-chandler and his family. Beastly creature, I know not what to do with him. Travel, quoth 'a! Ay, travel, travel, get thee gone, get thee but far enough, to the Saracens or the Tartars or the Turks, for thou are not fit to live in a Christian commonwealth, thou beastly pagan.

SIR WILFULL. Turks? No; no Turks, aunt: your Turks are infidels, and believe not in the grape. Your Mahometan, your Mussulman, is a dry stinkard – no offence, aunt. My map says that your Turk is not so honest a man as your Christian – I cannot find by the map that your Mufti is orthodox – whereby it is a plain case, that orthodox is a hard word, aunt, and (*Hiccup.*) Greek for claret. (*Sings.*)

> To drink is a Christian diversion,
> Unknown to the Turk and the Persian:

> Let Mahometan fools
> Live by heathenish rules,
> And be damned over tea cups and coffee!
> But let British lads sing,
> Crown a health to the king,
> And a fig for your Sultan and Sophy!

Ah Tony!

Enter FOIBLE, *and whispers* LADY WISHFORT.

LADY WISHFORT. Sir Rowland impatient? Good lack! what shall I do with this beastly tumbril? – Go lie down and sleep, you sot, or as I'm a person, I'll have you bastinadoed with broomsticks. Call up the wenches.

Exit FOIBLE.

SIR WILFULL. Ahey! Wenches, where are the wenches?

LADY WISHFORT. Dear cousin Witwoud, get him away, and you will bind me to you inviolably. I have an affair of moment that invades me with some precipitation. You will oblige me to all futurity.

WITWOUD. Come, knight. Pox on him, I don't know what to say to him. Will you go to a cock-match?

SIR WILFULL. With a wench, Tony? Is she a shakebag, sirrah? Let me bite your cheek for that.

WITWOUD. Horrible! He has a breath like a bagpipe. Ay, ay, come, will you march, my Salopian?

SIR WILFULL. Lead on, little Tony – I'll follow thee, my Anthony, my Tantony, sirrah, thou shalt be my Tantony, and I'll be thy pig.

And a fig for your Sultan and Sophy.

Exit singing with WITWOUD.

LADY WISHFORT. This will never do. It will never make a match at least before he has been abroad.

Enter WAITWELL, *disguised as* SIR ROWLAND.

Dear Sir Rowland, I am confounded with confusion at the retrospection of my own rudeness, I have more pardons to ask than the Pope distributes in the year of Jubilee. But I hope where there is likely to be so near an alliance, we may unbend the severity of decorum and dispense with a little ceremony.

WAITWELL. My impatience, madam, is the effect of my transport; and till I have the possession of your adorable person, I am tantalized on a rack, and do but hang, madam, on the tenter of expectation.

LADY WISHFORT. You have excess of gallantry, Sir Rowland, and press things to a conclusion with a most prevailing vehemence. But a day or two for decency of marriage –

WAITWELL. For decency of funeral, madam. The delay will break my heart – or if that should fail, I shall be poisoned. My nephew will get an inkling of my designs and poison me, and I would willingly starve him before I die – I would gladly go out of the world with that satisfaction. That would be some comfort to me, if I could but live so long as to be revenged on that unnatural viper.

LADY WISHFORT. Is he so unnatural say you? Truly I would contribute much both to the saving of your life and the accomplishment of your revenge. Not that I respect myself; though he has been a perfidious wretch to me.

WAITWELL. Perfidious to you!

LADY WISHFORT. Oh Sir Rowland, the hours that he has died away at my feet, the tears that he has shed, the oaths that he has sworn, the palpitations that he has felt, the trances, and the tremblings, the ardours and the ecstasies, the kneelings and the risings, the heart-heavings and the hand-grippings, the pangs and the pathetic regards of his protesting eyes! Oh, no memory can register.

WAITWELL. What, my rival! Is the rebel my rival? 'A dies.

LADY WISHFORT. No, don't kill him at once Sir Rowland, starve him gradually, inch by inch.

WAITWELL. I'll do't. In three weeks he shall be barefoot; in a
month out at knees with begging an alms. He shall starve
upward and upward, till he has nothing living but his head,
and then go out in a stink like a candle's end upon a save-all.

LADY WISHFORT. Well, Sir Rowland, you have the way. You
are no novice in the labyrinth of love; you have the clue. But as
I am a person, Sir Rowland, you must not attribute my yielding
to any sinister appetite, or indigestion of widowhood; nor
impute my complacency to any lethargy of continence. I hope
you do not think me prone to any iteration of nuptials –

WAITWELL. Far be it from me –

LADY WISHFORT. If you do, I protest I must recede – or think
that I have made a prostitution of decorums, but in the vehemence of compassion, and to save the life of a person of so
much importance

WAITWELL. I esteem it so

LADY WISHFORT. Or else you wrong my condescension

WAITWELL. I do not, I do not –

LADY WISHFORT. Indeed you do –

WAITWELL. I do not, fair shrine of virtue –

LADY WISHFORT. If you think the least scruple of carnality was
an ingredient –

WAITWELL. Dear madam, no. You are all camphire and
frankincense, all chastity and odour –

LADY WISHFORT. Or that –

Enter FOIBLE.

FOIBLE. Madam, the dancers are ready, and there's one with a
letter, who must deliver it into your own hands.

LADY WISHFORT. Sir Rowland, will you give me leave? Think
favourably, judge candidly, and conclude you have found a
person who would suffer racks in honour's cause, dear Sir
Rowland, and will wait on you incessantly. (*Exit.*)

WAITWELL. Fie, fie! What a slavery have I undergone. Spouse, hast thou any cordial? I want spirits.

FOIBLE. What a washy rogue art thou, to pant thus for a quarter of an hour's lying and swearing to a fine lady!

WAITWELL. Oh, she is the antidote to desire. Spouse, thou wilt fare the worse for't. I shall have no appetite to iteration of nuptials this eight-and-forty hours. By this hand I'd rather be a chairman in the dog-days than act Sir Rowland till this time tomorrow.

Enter LADY WISHFORT *with a letter.*

LADY WISHFORT. Call in the dancers. Sir Rowland, we'll sit if you please, and see the entertainment.

Dance.

Now with your permission Sir Rowland, I will peruse my letter. I would open it in your presence, because I would not make you uneasy. If it should make you uneasy, I would burn it. Speak, if it does – but you may see by the superscription it is like a woman's hand.

FOIBLE (*to him*). By heaven! Mrs Marwood's – I know it – my heart aches – get it from her.

WAITWELL. A woman's hand? No, madam, that's no woman's hand; I see that already. That's somebody whose throat must be cut.

LADY WISHFORT. Nay Sir Rowland, since you give me a proof of your passion by your jealousy, I promise you I'll make you a return, by a frank communication. You shall see it – we'll open it together. Look you here.

(*Reads.*) – Madam, though unknown to you (look you there, 'tis from nobody that I know) – I have that honour for your character, that I think myself obliged to let you know you are abused. He who pretends to be Sir Rowland is a cheat and a rascal –

Oh heavens! what's this?

FOIBLE. Unfortunate. All's ruined.

WAITWELL. How, how, let me see, let me see – (*Reading.*) A rascal, and disguised and suborned for that imposture – Oh villainy, Oh villainy! – by the contrivance of –

LADY WISHFORT. I shall faint, I shall die, I shall die, oh!

FOIBLE (*to him*). Say 'tis your nephew's hand – quickly – his plot, swear, swear it –

WAITWELL. Here s a villain! Madam, don't you perceive it, don't you see it?

LADY WISHFORT. Too well, too well! I have seen too much.

WAITWELL. I told you at first I knew the hand. A woman's hand? The rascal writes a sort of a large hand, your Roman hand. I saw there was a throat to be cut presently. If he were my son, as he is my nephew, I'd pistol him

FOIBLE. Oh treachery! But are you sure, Sir Rowland, it is his writing?

WAITWELL. Sure? Am I here? Do I live? Do I love this pearl of India? I have twenty letters in my pocket from him in the same character.

LADY WISHFORT. How!

FOIBLE. Oh, what luck it is, Sir Rowland, that you were present at this juncture! This was the business that brought Mr Mirabell disguised to Madam Millamant this afternoon. I thought something was contriving when he stole by me and would have hid his face.

LADY WISHFORT. How, how! I heard the villain was in the house indeed, and now I remember, my niece went away abruptly when Sir Wilfull was to have made his addresses.

FOIBLE' Then, then, madam, Mr Mirabell waited for her in her chamber; but I would not tell your ladyship to discompose you when you were to receive Sir Rowland.

WAITWELL. Enough! His date is short.

FOIBLE. No, good Sir Rowland, don't incur the law.

WAITWELL. Law? I care not for law. I can but die, and 'tis in a good cause. My lady shall be satisfied of my truth and innocence, though it cost me my life.

LADY WISHFORT. No, dear Sir Rowland, don't fight, if you should be killed I must never show my face, or be hanged. Oh, consider my reputation, Sir Rowland. No, you shan't fight. I'll go in and examine my niece; I'll make her confess. I conjure you Sir Rowland, by all your love, not to fight.

WAITWELL. I am charmed madam, I obey. But some proof you must let me give you; I'll go for a black box which contains the writings of my whole estate, and deliver that into your hands.

LADY WISHFORT. Ay, dear Sir Rowland, that will be some comfort; bring the black box.

WAITWELL. And may I presume to bring a contract to be signed this night? May I hope so far?

LADY WISHFORT. Bring what you will; but come alive, pray come alive. Oh this is a happy discovery.

WAITWELL. Dead or alive I'll come and married we will be in spite of treachery; ay, and get an heir that shall defeat the last remaining glimpse of hope in my abandoned nephew. Come, my buxom widow.

Ere long you shall substantial proof receive
That I'm an arrant knight –

FOIBLE (*aside*). Or arrant knave.

Exeunt.

ACT FIVE

Scene One

Scene continues.

LADY WISHFORT *and* FOIBLE.

LADY WISHFORT. Out of my house, out of my house, thou
viper, thou serpent, that I have fostered, thou bosom traitress,
that I raised from nothing – begone, begone, begone, go, go –
that I took from washing of old gauze and weaving of dead
hair, with a bleak blue nose, over a chafing-dish of starved
embers and dining behind a traverse rag, in a shop no bigger
than a bird-cage – go, go, starve again, do, do.

FOIBLE. Dear madam, I'll beg pardon on my knees.

LADY WISHFORT. Away, out, out! Go set up for yourself again –
do, drive a trade, do, with your three pennyworth of small
ware, flaunting upon a pack-thread, under a brandy-seller's
bulk, or against a dead wall by a ballad-monger. Go hang out
an old frisoneer gorget, with a yard of yellow colberteen again,
do. An old gnawed mask, two rows of pins and a child's fiddle;
a glass necklace with the beads broken, and a quilted night-
cap with one ear! Go, go, drive a trade – these were your
commodities, you treacherous trull, this was your merchandise
you dealt in when I took you into my house, placed you next
myself, and made you governante of my whole family. You
have forgot this, have you, now you have feathered your nest?

FOIBLE. No, no, dear madam. Do but hear me, have but a
moment's patience – I'll confess all. Mr Mirabell seduced me;
I am not the first that he has wheedled with his dissembling
tongue. Your ladyship's own wisdom has been deluded by him,

then how should I, a poor ignorant, defend myself? Oh madam, if you knew but what he promised me, and how he assured me your ladyship should come to no damage. Or else the wealth of the Indies should not have bribed me to conspire against so good, so sweet, so kind a lady as you have been to me.

LADY WISHFUL. 'No damage?' What, to betray me, to marry me to a cast serving-man; to make me a receptacle, an hospital for a decayed pimp? 'No damage?' Oh thou frontless impudence, more than a big-bellied actress.

FOIBLE. Pray do but hear me madam, he could not marry your ladyship, madam. No indeed, his marriage was to have been void in law, for he was married to me first, to secure your ladyship. He could not have bedded your ladyship; for if he had consummated with your ladyship, he must have run the risk of the law and been put upon his clergy. Yes indeed, I enquired of the law in that case before I would meddle or make.

LADY WISHFORT. What, then I have been your property, have I? I have been convenient to you it seems, while you were catering for Mirabell. I have been broker for you? What, have you made a passive bawd of me? This exceeds all precedent; I am brought to fine uses, to become a botcher of secondhand marriages between Abigails and Andrews! I'll couple you. Yes, I'll baste you together, you and your Philander. I'll Duke's Place you, as I'm a person. Your turtle is in custody already; you shall coo in the same cage, if there be constable or warrant in the parish.

Exit.

FOIBLE. Oh that ever I was born! Oh that I was ever married! A bride, ay, I shall be a Bridewell bride. Oh!

Enter MRS FAINALL.

MRS FAINALL. Poor Foible, what's the matter?

FOIBLE. Oh madam, my lady's gone for a constable; I shall be had to a justice, and put to Bridewell to beat hemp. Poor Waitwell's gone to prison already.

MRS FAINALL. Have a good heart, Foible; Mirabell's gone to give security for him. This is all Marwood's and my husband's doing.

FOIBLE. Yes, yes, I know it, madam. She was in my lady's closet, and overheard all that you said to me before dinner. She sent the letter to my lady, and that missing effect, Mr Fainall laid this plot to arrest Waitwell when he pretended to go for the papers; and in the meantime Mrs Marwood declared all to my lady.

MRS FAINALL. Was there no mention made of me in the letter? My mother does not suspect my being in the confederacy? I fancy Marwood has not told her, though she has told my husband.

FOIBLE. Yes, madam, but my lady did not see that part. We stifled the letter before she read so far. Has that mischievous devil told Mr Fainall of your ladyship then?

MRS FAINALL. Ay, all's out, my affair with Mirabell, everything discovered. This is the last day of our living together, that's my comfort.

FOIBLE. Indeed madam, and so 'tis a comfort if you knew all. He has been even with your ladyship; which I could have told you long enough since, but I love to keep peace and quietness by my good will; I had rather bring friends together than set 'em at distance. But Mrs Marwood and he are nearer related than ever their parents thought for.

MRS FAINALL. Say'st thou so, Foible? Canst thou prove this?

FOIBLE. I can take my oath of it, madam; so can Mrs Mincing. We have had many a fair word from Madam Marwood, to conceal something that passed in our chamber one evening when you were at Hyde Park and we were thought to have gone a-walking; but we went up unawares, though we were sworn to secrecy too. Madam Marwood took a book and swore us upon it; but it was but a book of verses and poems – so as long as it was not a Bible oath, we may break it with a safe conscience.

MRS FAINALL. This discovery is the most opportune thing
I could wish. Now, Mincing?

Enter MINCING.

MINCING. My lady would speak with Mrs Foible, mem. Mr
Mirabell is with her; he has set your spouse at liberty, Mrs
Foible, and would have you hide yourself in my lady's closet till
my old lady's anger is abated. Oh, my old lady is in a perilous
passion at something Mr Fainall has said. He swears, and my
old lady cries. There's a fearful hurricane, I vow. He says,
mem, how that he'll have my lady's fortune made over to
him, or he'll be divorced.

MRS FAINALL. Does your lady and Mirabell know that?

MINCING. Yes, mem; they have sent me to see if Sir Wilfull be
sober, and to bring him to them. My lady is resolved to have
him, I think, rather than lose such a vast sum as six thousand
pound. Oh, come Mrs Foible, I hear my old lady.

MRS FAINALL. Foible, you must tell Mincing that she must
prepare to vouch when I call her.

FOIBLE. Yes, yes madam.

MINCING. Oh yes, mem, I'll vouch anything for your ladyship's
service, be what it will.

Exeunt MINCING *and* FOIBLE.

Enter LADY WISHFORT *and* MARWOOD.

LADY WISHFORT. Oh my dear friend, how can I enumerate
the benefits that I have received from your goodness? To you
I owe the timely discovery of the false vows of Mirabell; to you
the detection of the impostor Sir Rowland. And now you are
become an intercessor with my son-in-law, to save the honour
of my house, and compound for the frailties of my daughter.
Well, friend, you are enough to reconcile me to the bad world,
or else I would retire to deserts and solitudes, and feed harmless
sheep by groves and purling streams. Dear Marwood, let us
leave the world, and retire by ourselves and be shepherdesses.

MRS MARWOOD. Let us first dispatch the affair in hand, madam; we shall have leisure to think of retirement afterwards. Here is one who is concerned in the treaty.

LADY WISHFORT. Oh daughter, daughter, is it possible thou shouldst be my child, bone of my bone, and flesh of my flesh, and as I may say, another me, and yet transgress the most minute particle of severe virtue? Is it possible you should lean aside to iniquity, who have been cast in the direct mould of virtue? I have not only been a mould but a pattern for you, and a model for you, after you were brought into the world.

MRS FAINALL. I don't understand your ladyship.

LADY WISHFORT. Not understand? Why, have you not been naught? Have you not been sophisticated? Not understand? Here I am ruined to compound for your caprices and your cuckoldoms. I must pawn my plate and my jewels and ruin my niece, and all little enough –

MRS FAINALL. I am wronged and abused, and so are you. 'Tis a false accusation, as false as hell, as false as your friend there, ay, or your friend's friend, my false husband.

MRS MARWOOD. My friend, Mrs Fainall? Your husband my friend? What do you mean?

MRS FAINALL. I know what I mean madam, and so do you; and so shall the world at a time convenient.

MRS MARWOOD. I am sorry to see you so passionate, madam. More temper would look more like innocence. But I have done. I am sorry my zeal to serve your ladyship and family should admit of misconstruction, or make me liable to affronts. You will pardon me, madam, if I meddle no more with an affair in which I am not personally concerned.

LADY WISHFORT. Oh dear friend, I am so ashamed that you should meet with such returns – you ought to ask pardon on your knees, ungrateful creature. She deserves more from you than all your life can accomplish. Oh, don't leave me destitute in this perplexity! No, stick to me, my good genius.

MRS FAINALL. I tell you, madam, you're abused. Stick to you? Ay, like a leech, to suck your best blood – she'll drop off when she's full. Madam, you shan't pawn a bodkin, nor part with a brass counter in composition for me. I defy 'em all. Let 'em prove their aspersions; I know my own innocence, and dare stand a trial. (*Exit.*)

LADY WISHFORT. Why, if she should be innocent, if she should be wronged after all, ha? I don't know what to think – and I promise you, her education has been unexceptionable. I may say it; for I chiefly made it my own care to initiate her very infancy in the rudiments of virtue, and to impress upon her tender years a young odium and aversion to the very sight of men. Ay, friend, she would ha' shrieked if she had but seen a man, till she was in her teens. As I'm a person 'tis true. She was never suffered to play with a male child, though but in coats; nay, her very babies were of the feminine gender. Oh, she never looked a man in the face but her own father, or the chaplain, and him we made a shift to put upon her for a woman, by the help of his long garments and his sleek face, till she was going in her fifteen.

MRS MARWOOD. 'Twas much she should be deceived so long.

LADY WISHFORT. I warrant you, or she would never have borne to have been catechized by him; and have heard his long lectures against singing and dancing, and such debaucheries, and going to filthy plays, and profane music meetings, where the lewd trebles squeak nothing but bawdy, and the bases roar blasphemy. Oh, she would have swooned at the sight or name of an obscene playbook and can I think after all this, that my daughter can be naught? What, a whore? And thought it excommunication to set her foot within the door of a playhouse. O my dear friend, I can't believe it, no, no. As she says, let him prove it, let him prove it.

MRS MARWOOD. Prove it madam? What, and have your name prostituted in a public court? Yours and your daughter's reputation worried at the bar by a pack of bawling lawyers? To be ushered in with an Oyez of scandal, and have your case opened by an old fumbling lecher in a quoif like a man-midwife to bring your daughter's infamy to light; to be a theme for legal punsters and quibblers by the statute, and become a jest against a rule of court, where there is no precedent for a jest in any record, not even in Doomsday Book; to discompose the gravity of the bench, and provoke naughty interrogatories in more naughty law Latin, while the good judge, tickled with the proceeding, simpers under a grey beard, and fidges off and on his cushion as if he had swallowed cantharides, or sat upon cow-itch.

LADY WISHFORT. Oh, tis very hard!

MRS MARWOOD. And then to have my young revellers of the Temple take notes, like 'prentices at a conventicle; and after, talk it all over again in commons, or before drawers in an eating-house.

LADY WISHFORT. Worse and worse.

MRS MARWOOD. Nay, this is nothing; if it would end here, 'twere well. But it must after this be consigned by the shorthand writers to the public press; and from thence be transferred to the hands, nay into the throats and lungs of hawkers, with voices more licentious than the loud flounderman's or the woman that cries 'grey peas'. And this you must hear till you are stunned; nay, you must hear nothing else for some days.

LADY WISHFORT. Oh, 'tis insupportable! No, no, dear friend, make it up, make it up; ay, ay, I'll compound. I'll give up all, myself and my all, my niece and her all, − anything, everything for composition.

MRS MARWOOD. Nay madam, I advise nothing, I only lay before you as a friend the inconveniencies which perhaps you have overseen. Here comes Mr Fainall. If he will be satisfied to huddle up all in silence, I shall be glad. You must think I would rather congratulate than condole with you.

Enter FAINALL.

LADY WISHFORT. Ay, ay, I do not doubt it, dear Marwood; no, no, I do not doubt it.

FAINALL. Well, madam, I have suffered myself to be overcome by the importunity of this lady your friend, and am content you shall enjoy your own proper estate during life, on condition you oblige yourself never to marry, under such penalty as I think convenient.

LADY WISHFORT. Never to marry?

FAINALL. No more Sir Rowlands – the next imposture may not be so timely detected.

MRS MARWOOD. That condition, I dare answer, my lady will consent to without difficulty; she has already but too much experienced the perfidiousness of men. Besides, madam, when we retire to our pastoral solitude, we shall bid adieu to all other thoughts.

LADY WISHFORT. Ay, that's true; but in case of necessity, as of health, or some such emergency –

FAINALL. Oh, if you are prescribed marriage, you shall be considered; I will only reserve to myself the power to choose for you. If your physic be wholesome, it matters not who is your apothecary. Next, my wife shall settle on me the remainder of her fortune not made over already, and for her maintenance depend entirely on my discretion.

LADY WISHFORT. This is most inhumanly savage, exceeding the barbarity of a Muscovite husband.

FAINALL. I learned it from his Czarish majesty's retinue, in a winter evening's conference over brandy and pepper, amongst other secrets of matrimony and policy, as they are at present practised in the northern hemisphere. But this must be agreed unto, and that positively. Lastly, I will be endowed, in right of my wife, with that six thousand pound which is the moiety of Mrs Millamant's fortune in your possession; and which she has forfeited (as will appear by the last will and testament of your deceased husband, Sir Jonathan Wishfort) by her disobedience in contracting herself against your consent or knowledge, and by refusing the offered match with Sir Wilfull Witwoud, which you, like a careful aunt, had provided for her.

LADY WISHFORT. My nephew was *non compos*, and could not make his addresses.

FAINALL. I come to make demands. I'll hear no objections.

LADY WISHFORT. You will grant me time to consider.

FAINALL. Yes, while the instrument is drawing, to which you must set your hand till more sufficient deeds can be perfected; which I will take care shall be done with all possible speed. In the meanwhile, I will go for the said instrument, and till my return, you may balance this matter in your own discretion.

Exit FAINALL.

LADY WISHFORT. This insolence is beyond all precedent, all parallel; must I be subject to this merciless villain?

MRS MARWOOD. 'Tis severe indeed, madam, that you should smart for your daughter's wantonness.

LADY WISHFORT. 'Twas against my consent that she married this barbarian, but she would have him, though her year was not out. Ah! her first husband, my son Languish, would not have carried it thus. Well, that was my choice, this is hers; she is matched now with a witness. I shall be mad; dear friend, is there no comfort for me? Must I live to be confiscated at this rebel rate? Here come two more of my Egyptian plagues too.

Enter MILLAMANT *and* SIR WILFULL.

SIR WILFULL. Aunt, your servant.

LADY WISHFORT. Out caterpillar, call not me aunt; I know thee not.

SIR WILFULL. I confess I have been a little in disguise, as they say. 'S'heart! and I'm sorry for't. What would you have? I hope I committed no offence, aunt, and if I did, I am willing to make satisfaction; and what can a man say fairer? If I have broke anything, I'll pay for't, an it cost a pound. And so let that content for what's past, and make no more words. For what's to come, to pleasure you I'm willing to marry my cousin. So pray let's all be friends, she and I are agreed upon the matter before a witness.

LADY WISHFORT. How's this, dear niece? Have I any comfort? Can this be true?

MILLAMANT. I am content to be a sacrifice to your repose, madam; and to convince you that I had no hand in the plot, as you were misinformed, I have laid my commands on Mirabell to come in person, and be a witness that I give my hand to this flower of knighthood; and for the contract that passed between Mirabell and me, I have obliged him to make a resignation of it, in your ladyship's presence. He is without, and waits your leave for admittance.

LADY WISHFORT. Well, I'll swear I am something revived at this testimony of your obedience; but I cannot admit that traitor. I fear I cannot fortify myself to support his appearance. He is as terrible to me as a Gorgon; if I see him, I fear I shall turn to stone, petrify incessantly.

MILLAMANT. If you disoblige him, he may resent your refusal and insist upon the contract still. Then 'tis the last time he will be offensive to you.

LADY WISHFORT. Are you sure it will be the last time? If I were sure of that. Shall I never see him again?

MILLAMANT. Sir Wilfull, you and he are to travel together, are you not?

SIR WILFULL. 'S'heart, the gentleman's a civil gentleman, aunt; let him come in. Why, we are sworn brothers and fellow travellers. We are to be Pylades and Orestes, he and I. He is to be my interpreter in foreign parts. He has been overseas once already; and with proviso that I marry my cousin will cross 'em once again, only to bear me company. 'S'heart, I'll call him in – an I set on't once, he shall come in; and see who'll hinder him. (*Exit.*)

MRS MARWOOD. This is precious fooling, if it would pass, but I'll know the bottom of it.

LADY WISHFORT. O dear Marwood, you are not going?

MARWOOD. Not far, madam; I'll return immediately. (*Exit.*)

Re-enter SIR WILFULL *and* MIRABELL.

SIR WILFULL. Look up man, I'll stand by you; 'sbud an she do frown, she can't kill you. Besides, harkee, she dare not frown desperately, because her face is none of her own. 'S'heart, an she should, her forehead would wrinkle like the coat of a cream-cheese, but mum for that, fellow traveller.

MIRABELL. If a deep sense of the many injuries I have offered to so good a lady, with a sincere remorse, and a hearty contrition, can but obtain the least glance of compassion I am too happy. Ah madam, there was a time – but let it be forgotten. I confess I have deservedly forfeited the high place I once held, of sighing at your feet. Nay, kill me not by turning from me in disdain; I come not to plead for favour; nay, not for pardon. I am a suppliant only for your pity. I am going where I never shall behold you more

SIR WILFULL. How, fellow traveller! You shall go by yourself then.

MIRABELL. Let me be pitied first, and afterwards forgotten – I ask no more.

SIR WILFULL. By'r Lady, a very reasonable request, and will cost you nothing, aunt. Come, come, forgive and forget, aunt, why you must, an you are a Christian.

MIRABELL. Consider, madam, in reality you could not receive much prejudice; it was an innocent device; though I confess it had a face of guiltiness. It was at most an artifice which love contrived, and errors which love produces have ever been accounted venial. At least think it is punishment enough that I have lost what in my heart I hold most dear, that to your cruel indignation I have offered up this beauty, and with her my peace and quiet; nay, all my hopes of future comfort.

SIR WILFULL. An he does not move me, would I might never be o' the Quorum. An it were not as good a deed as to drink, to give her to him again, I would I might never take shipping. Aunt, if you don't forgive quickly, I shall melt, I can tell you that. My contract went no further than a little mouth-glue, and that's hardly dry; one doleful sigh more from my fellow traveller, and 'tis dissolved.

LADY WISHFORT. Well, nephew, upon your account – ah, he has a false insinuating tongue! Well, sir, I will stifle my just resentment at my nephew's request. I will endeavour what I can to forget, but on proviso that you resign the contract with my niece immediately.

MIRABELL. It is in writing, and with papers of concern; but I have sent my servant for it, and will deliver it to you, with all acknowledgments for your transcendent goodness.

LADY WISHFORT (*aside*). Oh, he has witchcraft in his eyes and tongue! When I did not see him, I could have bribed a villain to his assassination; but his appearance rakes the embers which have so long lain smothered in my breast.

Enter FAINALL *and* MRS MARWOOD.

FAINALL. Your date of deliberation, madam, is expired. Here is the instrument; are you prepared to sign?

LADY WISHFORT. If I were prepared, I am not empowered. My niece exerts a lawful claim, having matched herself by my direction to Sir Wilfull.

FAINALL. That sham is too gross to pass on me, though 'tis imposed on you, madam.

MILLAMANT. Sir, I have given my consent.

MIRABELL. And, sir, I have resigned my pretensions.

SIR WILFULL. And, sir, I assert my right; and will maintain it in defiance of you, sir, and of your instrument. 'S'heart an you talk of an instrument, sir, I have an old fox by my thigh shall hack your instrument of ram vellum to shreds, sir! It shall not be sufficient for a mittimus or a tailor's measure. Therefore withdraw your instrument, sir, or by'r Lady, I shall draw mine.

LADY WISHFORT. Hold nephew, hold.

MILLAMANT. Good Sir Wilfull, respite your valour.

FAINALL. Indeed? Are you provided of a guard, with your single Beefeater there? But I'm prepared for you, and insist upon my first proposal. You shall submit your own estate to my management, and absolutely make over my wife's to my sole use, as pursuant to the purport and tenor of this other covenant. (*To* MILLAMANT.) I suppose, madam, your consent is not requisite in this case; nor, Mr Mirabell, your resignation; nor, Sir Wilfull, your right. You may draw your fox if you please, sir, and make a bear-garden flourish somewhere else, for here it will not avail. This, my Lady Wishfort, must be subscribed, or your darling daughter's turned adrift, like a leaky hulk to sink or swim, as she and the current of this lewd town can agree.

LADY WISHFORT. Is there no means, no remedy, to stop my ruin? Ungrateful wretch! Dost thou not owe thy being, thy subsistence, to my daughter's fortune?

FAINALL. I'll answer you when I have the rest of it in my possession.

MIRABELL. But that you would not accept of a remedy from my hands – I own I have not deserved you should owe any obligation to me; or else perhaps I could advise –

LADY WISHFORT. Oh what? what? To save me and my child from ruin, from want, I'll forgive all that's past; nay I'll consent to anything to come, to be delivered from this tyranny.

MIRABELL. Ay, madam; but that is too late, my reward is intercepted. You have disposed of her who only could have made me a compensation for all my services. But be it as it may, I am resolved I'll serve you; you shall not be wronged in this savage manner.

LADY WISHFORT. How! Dear Mr Mirabell, can you be so generous at last? But it is not possible. Harkee, I'll break my nephew's match; you shall have my niece yet, and all her fortune, if you can but save me from this imminent danger.

MIRABELL. Will you? I take you at your word. I ask no more. I must have leave for two criminals to appear.

LADY WISHFORT. Ay, ay, anybody, anybody.

MIRABELL. Foible is one, and a penitent.

Enter MRS FAINALL, FOIBLE, *and* MINCING.

MRS MARWOOD (*to* FAINALL). Oh my shame! (MIRABELL *and* LADY WISHFORT *go to* MRS FAINALL *and* FOIBLE.) These corrupt things are bought and brought hither to expose me.

FAINALL. If it must all come out, why let 'em know it, tis but the way of the world. That shall not urge me to relinquish or abate one tittle of my terms; no, I will insist the more.

FOIBLE. Yes indeed, madam; I'll take my Bible oath of it.

MINCING. And so will I, mem.

LADY WISHFORT. Oh Marwood, Marwood, art thou false? My friend deceive me? Hast thou been a wicked accomplice with that profligate man?

MRS MARWOOD. Have you so much ingratitude and injustice, to give credit against your friend to the aspersions of two such mercenary trulls?

MINCING. 'Mercenary', mem? I scorn your words. 'Tis true we found you and Mr Fainall in the blue garret; by the same token, you swore us to secrecy upon Messalina's poems. 'Mercenary?' No, if we would have been mercenary, we should have held our tongues; you would have bribed us sufficiently.

FAINALL. Go, you are an insignificant thing. Well, what are you the better for this? Is this Mr Mirabell's expedient? I'll be put off no longer. You thing, that was a wife, shall smart for this. I will not leave thee wherewithal to hide thy shame. Your body shall be naked as your reputation.

MRS FAINALL. I despise you and defy your malice. You have
aspersed me wrongfully. I have proved your falsehood. Go
you and your treacherous – I will not name it – but starve
together – perish.

FAINALL. Not while you are worth a groat. Indeed my dear
madam, I'll be fooled no longer.

LADY WISHFORT. Ah Mr Mirabell, this is small comfort, the
detection of this affair.

MIRABELL. Oh, in good time. Your leave for the other offender
and penitent to appear, madam.

Enter WAITWELL *with a box of writings.*

LADY WISHFORT. Oh, Sir Rowland! Well, rascal?

WAITWELL. What your ladyship pleases. I have brought the
black box at last, madam.

MIRABELL. Give it me. Madam, you remember your promise.

LADY WISHFORT. Ay, dear sir.

MIRABELL. Where are the gentlemen?

WAITWELL. At hand sir, rubbing their eyes; just risen from sleep.

FAINALL. 'Sdeath, what's this to me? I'll not wait your private
concerns.

Enter PETULANT *and* WITWOUD.

PETULANT. How now? What's the matter? Whose hand's out?

WITWOUD. Heyday! What, are you all got together, like players
at the end of the last act?

MIRABELL. You may remember, gentlemen, I once requested
your hands as witnesses to a certain parchment.

WITWOUD. Ay, I do, my hand I remember. Petulant set his mark.

MIRABELL. You wrong him, his name is fairly written, as shall
appear. You do not remember, gentlemen, anything of what
that parchment contained?

Undoing the box.

WITWOUD. No.

PETULANT. Not I. I writ. I read nothing.

MIRABELL. Very well; now you shall know. Madam, your promise.

LADY WISHFORT. Ay, ay, sir, upon my honour.

MIRABELL. Mr Fainall, it is now time that you should know that your lady, while she was at her own disposal, and before you had by your insinuations wheedled her out of a pretended settlement of the greatest part of her fortune –

FAINALL. Sir! Pretended!

MIRABELL. Yes, sir. I say that this lady while a widow, having it seems received some cautions respecting your inconstancy and tyranny of temper, which from her own partial opinion and fondness of you, she could never have suspected – she did, I say, by the wholesome advice of friends and of sages learned in the laws of this land, deliver this same as her act and deed to me in trust, and to the uses within mentioned. You may read if you please (*Holding out the parchment.*) though perhaps what is inscribed on the back may serve your occasions.

FAINALL. Very likely, sir. What's here? Damnation! (*Reads.*) A deed of conveyance of the whole estate real of Arabella Languish, widow, in trust to Edward Mirabell. Confusion!

MIRABELL. Even so, sir; 'tis the way of the world, sir, of the widows of the world. I suppose this deed may bear an elder date than what you have obtained from your lady.

FAINALL. Perfidious fiend! Then thus I'll be revenged. (*Offers to run at* MRS FAINALL.)

SIR WILFULL. Hold, sir, now you may make your bear-garden flourish somewhere else, sir.

FAINALL. Mirabell, you shall hear of this, sir; be sure you shall. Let me pass, oaf!

Exit.

MRS FAINALL. Madam, you seem to stifle your resentment; you had better give it vent.

MRS MARWOOD. Yes, it shall have vent – and to your confusion, or I'll perish in the attempt.

Exit.

LADY WISHFORT. Oh daughter, daughter, 'tis plain thou hast inherited thy mother's prudence.

MRS FAINALL. Thank Mr Mirabell, a cautious friend, to whose advice all is owing.

LADY WISHFORT. Well, Mr Mirabell, you have kept your promise, and I must perform mine. First, I pardon for your sake, Sir Rowland there, and Foible. The next thing is to break the matter to my nephew – and how to do that –

MIRABELL. For that, madam, give yourself no trouble; let me have your consent. Sir Wilfull is my friend; he has had compassion upon lovers and generously engaged a volunteer in this action, for our service, and now designs to prosecute his travels.

SIR WILFULL. 'S'heart aunt, I have no mind to marry. My cousin's a fine lady, and the gentleman loves her and she loves him, and they deserve one another. My resolution is to see foreign parts. I have set on't – and when I'm set on't, I must do't. And if these two gentlemen would travel too, I think they may be spared.

PETULANT. For my part, I say little – I think things are best off or on.

WITWOUD. Egad I understand nothing of the matter – I'm in a maze yet, like a dog in a dancing school.

LADY WISHFORT. Well sir, take her, and with her all the joy I can give you.

MILLAMANT. Why does not the man take me? Would you have me give myself to you over again.

MIRABELL. Ay, and over and over again; for I would have you as often as possibly I can. (*Kisses her hand.*) Well, heaven grant I love you not too well, that's all my fear.

SIR WILFULL. 'S'heart, you'll have him time enough to toy after you're married; or, if you will toy now, let us have a dance in the meantime, that we who are not lovers may have some other employment besides looking on.

MIRABELL. With all my heart, dear Sir Wilfull. What shall we do for music?

FOIBLE. Oh, sir, some that were provided for Sir Rowland's entertainment are yet within call.

A dance.

LADY WISHFORT. As I am a person I can hold out no longer. I have wasted my spirits so today already that I am ready to sink under the fatigue; and I cannot but have some fears upon me yet that my son Fainall will pursue some desperate course.

MIRABELL. Madam, disquiet not yourself on that account. To my knowledge his circumstances are such, he must of force comply. For my part, I will contribute all that in me lies to a reunion. (*To* MRS FAINALL.) In the meantime, madam, let me before these witnesses restore to you this deed of trust. It may be a means, well managed, to make you live easily together.

From hence let those be warned, who mean to wed,
Lest mutual falsehood stain the bridal bed;
For each deceiver to his cost may find,
That marriage frauds too oft are paid in kind.

Exeunt omnes.

Epilogue

Spoken by Mrs Bracegirdle.

After our epilogue this crowd dismisses,
I'm thinking how this play'll be pulled to pieces.
But pray consider ere you doom its fall,
How hard a thing 'twould be to please you all.
There are some critics so with spleen diseased,
They scarcely come inclining to be pleased;
And sure he must have more than mortal skill,
Who pleases anyone against his will.
Then, all bad poets we are sure, are foes,
And how their number's swelled the town well knows;
In shoals I've marked 'em judging in the pit;
Though they're on no pretence for judgment fit,
But that they have been damned for want of wit.
Since when, they, by their own offences taught,
Set up for spies on plays, and finding fault.
Others there are whose malice we'd prevent;
Such who watch plays with scurrilous intent
To mark out who by characters are meant.
And though no perfect likeness they can trace,
Yet each pretends to know the copied face.
These with false glosses feed their own ill nature,
And turn to libel, what was meant a satire.
May such malicious fops this fortune find,
To think themselves alone the fools designed;
If any are so arrogantly vain,
To think they singly can support a scene,
And furnish fool enough to entertain.
For well the learned and the judicious know,
That satire scorns to stoop so meanly low

As any one abstracted fop to show.
For, as when painters form a matchless face,
They from each fair one catch some different grace,
And shining features in one portrait blend,
To which no single beauty must pretend;
So poets oft do in one piece expose
Whole *belles assemblées* of coquettes and beaux.

   Finis.

GLOSSARY

Abigails and Andrews – female and male servants

angle into Blackfriars with a mitten – prisoners would fish for offerings
   from passers-by by letting down a mitten on a string

assafoetida – a strong smelling medicine

atlases – silk-satins

babies – dolls

Baldwin – a traditional name for an ass

Barbadoes waters – a type of brandy

Bartlemew and his fair – the great fair held on St Bartholomew's Day
   was notorious for its freak shows

borachio – a drunkard

Bridewell – a prison

bubbles – dupes

bulk – stall

bum baily – 'a bailiff of the meanest kind; one employed in arrests'
   (Dr Johnson's *Dictionary*)

buttered – flattered

B'w'y – [God] be with you

Bunyan – John Bunyan, Puritan author of *Pilgrim's Progress*

burnishes – fattens

canonical hours – the hours during which legal marriages could
   take place

call of serjeants – a group of barristers who qualified together

camphire – camphor

cantharides – Spanish Fly, an aphrodisiac

cap of maintenance – in heraldry, a cap with two points like horns.
   Part of a series of jokes about the horns traditionally associated
   with cuckolds

catering – procuring

chair-man – sedan chair carrier

chemist – alchemist

to choose – by choice

clary – a type of brandy

colberteen – a type of lace

commonplace – a book in which noteworthy quotations are entered

commons – communal meals

condition – high status

coventicle – a meeting of religious Dissenters

cow-itch – a stinging plant

crips – an obsolete or (given the speaker) affected form of 'crisp'

Dame Partlet – wife of the cock Chanticleer in fables

Dawk's Letter – a newspaper

decimo sexto – (Latin) a very small book, one with each sheet folded into sixteen pages, whereas a folio has one fold

deputy-lieutenant's hall – presumably full of mounted stag's heads. Part of a series of jokes about the horns traditionally associated with cuckolds

doily – a light material

dormitives – sleep-inducing drinks

douceurs – (French) sweetnesses

drap-du-Berry – coarse cloth from Berry in France

drawer – waiter

Duke's Place – location of a church where irregular marriages took place

l'étourdie – (French) the giddy town

exceptious – inclined to take exception

fadler – fondler

fidges – fidgets

fishmonger hates a hard frost – since ice makes fishing difficult

fit – an affected pronunciation of 'fought'

fox – sword

flapdragon – a raisin in the game of the same name

frippery – worn out clothes

frisoneer gorget – a type of neck cover

frontless – shameless

Furnivall's Inn – one of the Inns of Court

gemini – twins

grutch – begrudge

incontinently – immediately

inprimis – (Latin) in the first place. A legal term

'I prithee spare me – first line of a poem by Sir John Suckling. Quoted by Millamant

Jubilee – a year in which the Pope offers special dispensations of punishments for sins

Lacedemonian – Spartan, with reference to their traditional brevity

Lelius – a patron of the Latin dramatist Terence

'Like Phoebus . . . – a line from Waller's *The Story of Phoebus and Daphne, Applied*

Locket's – a well-known tavern

Long Lane penthouse – a stall in a road notorious for its rag pedlars

Ludgate – Ludgate debtors' prison

medlar grafted on a crab – a type of apple eaten when mushy through decay grafted on to a sour wild apple eaten when hard

Menander – a Greek dramatist

Messalina's poems – probably Mincing's mistake for a 'miscellany of poems', but very appropriate since the historical Messalina was notorious for her sexual activities

mittimus – (Latin) a warrant for imprisonment

moiety – half

Montague – Ralph Montague (1638- 1709), politician and courtier who made two fortunes by marriage

month's mind – strong desire

Mopus – stupid person

Mosca in The Fox – Volpone's accomplice in Jonson's *Volpone*

Mrs Engine – Mrs Trickery

Mufti – Muslim priest

noli prosequi – (Latin) phrase used to end legal proceedings

olio – a mixture, from a Spanish stew with varied ingredients

Ordinary – the prison chaplain

pack-thread – twine ('flaunting upon a pack-thread' may mean living on a shoestring or could refer to prostitution)

Pam – the highest card in the game of Loo

Pancras – a church where irregular marriages took place

Partlet – the wife of Chanticleer the Cock in Chaucer's *Nun's Priest's Tale*

Penthesilea – Queen of the Amazons

peruke – wig

Philander – lover

pieced – enlarged

projection – the last stage of making base metal into gold in alchemy

Prynne – William Prynne, author of *Histriomastix*, a Puritan attack on the theatre

Pumplenose – Pimplenose

pulvilled – perfumed with powder

put upon his clergy – criminals who could read and write could claim 'benefit of clergy' to escape the death penalty

Pylades and Orestes – representative faithful friends

Quarles – Francis Quarles, a theological controversialist

quoif – a lawyer's cap

Quorum – to be 'o'the Quorum' means to be a Justice of the Peace

rantipole – ill mannered

ratafia – a type of brandy

Rekin – the Wrekin, a famous hill in Shropshire

Rosamond's Pond – a meeting place in St James's Park

Roxalana – the wife of the Sultan in William Davenant's *The Siege of Rhodes*

Salop – Shropshire

save-all – a type of candle holder

Scipio – a patron of the Latin dramatist Terence

shake-bag – a kind of fighting cock

smoke – mock

sommeils du matin – morning drowsinesses

sophisticated – corrupted

Sophy – a Persian ruler

Spanish paper – used for applying rouge

strait-lacing – tight corseting

Strammel – a gaunt person

Suckling – Sir John Suckling, the poet. Sir Wilfull thinks he is being called a young pig

tallow-chandler – a manufacturer and seller of candles made from tallow

Tantony – shortened form of St Antony, who is often depicted with a pig

Theophrastus – ancient Greek author of *Characters*

'*There never yet . . .* – first line of a poem by Sir John Suckling.
    Quoted by Millamant
'*Thyrsis a youth* – first line of Edmund Waller's *The Story of Phoebus
    and Daphne, Applied.* Quoted by Millamant
tift – arranged
Truewit – a character in Jonson's *Epicene*
turtles – turtle doves, birds associated with love
unsized camlet – unstiffened material
watch-night – night light
weekly bill – the weekly record of deaths in the City of London
whim it about – spin
with a witness – with a vengeance
worse than a quaker hates a parrot – since a quaker's sober dress and
    behaviour are seen as contrasting sharply with the noise and
    colour of a parrot
[*he*]*r year* – year of mourning